Defeating Procrastination

Defeating Procrastination

52 Fail-Safe Tips for
Keeping Time on Your Side

Marlene Caroselli, Ed.D.

SkillPath Publications
Mission, KS

Editor: Kelly Scanlon

Copyeditor: Mason Cole

Page Layout: Premila Malik Borchardt

Cover Design: Rod Hankins

Library of Congress Catalog Card Number: 96-69847

ISBN: 1-57294-078-6

10 9 8 7 6 5 4 3 2 1   97   98   99   00   01

Printed in the United States of America

Contents

Introduction

Here is a vivid example of the viciousness of the procrastination monster:

- Investor "A" put away $200 a month for 10 years, earning a return of 8 percent per year, resulting in a total investment of $24,000.

- Investor "B" put away $200 a month for 20 years, earning a rate of 8 percent per year, resulting in an investment of $48,000.

- The basic difference—other than an additional ten years of investing and an additional $24,000 investment—is that Investor "B" started ten years *after* Investor "A."

Over the thirty-year period, the investments look like this:

# Years	Investor "A"	Investor "B"
30	-0-	$24,000
20	-0-	$24,000
10	$24,000	-0-

During the thirty-year period, "A" left his money dormant for the last twenty years. "B" didn't invest at all for the first ten years but did for the next twenty. At the end of the thirty-year period, the two investment totals were the following:

$114, 532 and *$168,991*

Which investor had which amount?

"A" earned over $50,000 more than "B," even though "A" invested half as much and did not invest at all in the last twenty years. There is no more telling a statistic than this to prove the dangers and damages that lie in wait for the procrastinator!

In *Defeating Procrastination*, you will receive one tool each week for overcoming procrastination and learning how to put time back on your side.

Don't believe for a moment that circumstances are beyond your control. You have the ability to do the things that need doing, despite what may be happening around you. If your environment is one of "management by crisis" or if management is always in a fire-fighting mode (such organizations do exist), either work with others to stabilize the situation or think about getting out. Sooner or later, you will be burned—or burned out!

Pledge now to use one idea a week for a whole year. Date the pages so you can see your own progress and feel compelled to continue. You're bound to notice an improvement in the way you get things done. In addition to the weekly weapons, you will find quotes, questions, and quizzes to inspire, prod, and force you to look at your current habits.

Defeating procrastination means giving up some of your old (bad) habits and acquiring new ones. This goal is a challenging one, but improvement is always a challenge. Commit to that challenge now by signing the following pledge:

I,_____, hereby acknowledge
    (print your name here)
my desire to defeat procrastination and thus increase my personal and professional efficiency. By committing to a weekly program, I pledge to develop new skills and refine old ones. I also take responsibility for practicing these skills each week (actually using the tools presented in this book) so I can develop new habits—at least ten from the fifty-two offered. I realize these new habits can lessen the stress produced by procrastination and can aid me in doing my work more carefully and proficiently.

_____
(sign your name here)

_____
(date)

Read on to learn how to take the "ow" out of "now."

Week 1:
Make a list of things to do.

Arthur Miller: "The word 'now' is like a bomb through the window, and it ticks."

You can lessen the tension procrastination produces by listing the things that need to be done. Instead of experiencing the vague uneasiness unspecified pressures create, you can use the list to define the realities of the tasks before you (which are usually not as great as you originally feared). Just list your obligations—as quickly as they come to mind—in no special order or priority. (Be sure to number the items on the list.) Then cross off items as you complete them. You're bound to feel the satisfaction of accomplishment. Do a list like this—whether or not you prioritize it—every single day and carry over the uncompleted tasks from one day to the next.

Make a separate list of the things you want to do when you find time. These are long-range projects or even fun activities, but they don't belong on the first list of responsibilities.

Also make a list of things you realize you have misplaced, rather than stopping what you are doing to go on a hunt. If you urgently need the item, of course, you have to stop to locate it. Otherwise, just put it on your list. Sooner or later, the missing item will turn up, or you'll locate it because you're more aware it's missing.

Action Questions

1. What kinds of things do you typically write down? (What kinds of lists do you keep?)

_____

_____

_____

_____

_____

_____

_____

2. From a psychological viewpoint, what is the benefit of keeping lists?

_____

_____

_____

_____

_____

_____

_____

Do It Now!

Place each of the numbered items on your list of things to do in one of the following quadrants.

Critical and needs immediate attention	Critical but does not need immediate attention
Needs immediate attention but not critical	**Not critical and does not need immediate attention**

Week 2:
Do the least appealing tasks first.

Mark Twain: "If you have to swallow a frog, don't stare at it too long!"

Although you may be tempted to do the "fun stuff" early and build a feeling of accomplishment, the "fun stuff" is seldom the stuff of which corporate dreams or missions are made. Usually the most difficult assignments have the biggest payoff. The ones people avoid doing often have a critical role in the flow of work.

Filing, for example, is often stacked in the "file pile," which grows daily. But if your boss needs an important document that's buried somewhere in the paper mountain on your desk, you may be doing harm to your career. Both your efficiency and your reputation suffer when you can't locate the papers that office operations depend on. And despite earlier predictions of "paperless societies," technology has not yet eliminated the need for hard copies.

Action Questions

1. Do you consciously try to get your least favorite task out of the way early, or do you allow it to hang over your head and haunt you all day long?

   _____

   _____

2. Other than relief, what are the benefits of completing the least-favored task early in the day?

   _____

   _____

   _____

   _____

3. What are your least favorite tasks?

   _____

   _____

   _____

4. Why do you dislike them?

   _____

   _____

   _____

5. Does anyone else enjoy doing them? If so, could you exchange tasks with that person?

   _____

   _____

   _____

Do It Now!

This game of "Least Favorite Tasks" is bound to produce both synergy and smiles as you involve your co-workers. Don't be fooled, however. While this activity is nearly as much fun as guessing whose baby picture belongs to what adult face, you *will* benefit quite a bit from it.

Ask each person in your office (including your supervisor) to write, anonymously, a brief description of the least favorite task he or she is required to do. Collect all the items, number them, and type up the entire list. Then have a contest to see who comes closest to matching the tasks with the people who wrote them. The "prize" could be a small token (such as a single rose that only costs a few dollars), or it could be having others do the winner's least favorite task for one whole week.

The list, however, should stimulate discussion in the office. Perhaps some of the tasks could be streamlined, combined with other tasks, or eliminated altogether. Also, it's possible that two employees could trade off. (As garage-salers know, one person's junk is another person's treasure.)

Week 3:
Prioritize.

Malcolm Forbes: "There is never enough time, unless you're serving it."

You've no doubt experienced days during which, it seemed, you were busy every single minute. And yet, at the end of the day when you asked yourself, "What exactly did I accomplish today?" the answer was a disappointing, "Very little."

The usual explanation for this is a failure to prioritize. Yes, you worked hard, but you didn't work hard toward primary goals. The Pareto Principle says that 20 percent of the things we do cause 80 percent of the effect. In other words, of all you have to do, usually only one thing in five is critical. So critical, in fact, that it produces 80 percent of the results. The remaining four items combined produce the remaining 20 percent of the outcomes.

By prioritizing, you can determine which are the most important tasks to be done each day.

Action Questions

1. If you don't prioritize on a daily basis, why not?

_____

_____

_____

_____

_____

2. If you do prioritize, what criteria do you use to determine the importance of each task?

_____

_____

_____

_____

_____

_____

_____

_____

Do It Now!

Make a list of all the things you do on a typical day.

_____

_____

_____

_____

_____

_____

_____

_____

_____

_____

_____

Now go back and prioritize, using the following system (or one of your own choosing):

- Place three stars and the letter "B" beside those the boss wants done right away.

- Place two stars and the letters "IC" beside those that internal customers need done.

- Place one star and the letter "P" beside those which, if not attended to on a timely basis, could create problems.

Prioritizing is nothing more than keeping a running tally of what has to be done by when.

Week 4:
Force yourself.

Emily Bronte: "A person who has not done one half his day's work by ten o'clock runs a chance of leaving the other half undone."

An "attitude of gratitude" will help you face procrastination. Whatever it is you have to do, the very fact that you *have* it to do says a number of things about you:

- You are physically able to work.

- You have a good mind.

- You have choices.

When you take the time to think about your own good fortune, the work that you postpone doing suddenly seems worth doing. You realize that you're lucky to have such work to do. Keeping these thoughts in mind is often enough stimulus for you to get up and get on with it.

Action Questions

1. Under what circumstances do you willingly want to tackle projects?

_____

_____

_____

_____

_____

_____

2. Which of those circumstances could be transferred to the least pleasant tasks that face you?

_____

_____

_____

_____

_____

_____

Do It Now!

Respond to the following statements by placing one check mark on the left of the continuum if the statement is untrue for you. In other words, if the statement does not resemble you at all, if it is "way off" in describing you, use one checkmark. If the statement relates to you in some ways, place two checkmarks in the middle of the continuum. If the statement is so true that you are actually experiencing benefits or payoffs, place three checkmarks on the right side of the continuum.

1. *I regard myself as a disciplined person.*

Way off	In some ways/on some days	Payoff

2. *When things go wrong, I look inside myself first rather than blame others.*

Way off	In some ways/on some days	Payoff

3. *I pride myself on being on top of things.*

Way off	In some ways/on some days	Payoff

4. *Others compliment me for having things in control.*

Way off	In some ways/on some days	Payoff

5. *I use some tricks to help me accomplish less enjoyable tasks.*

Way off	In some ways/on some days	Payoff

How did you do?

If you had only one or two three-check answers, it's time to examine your approach to work and to get help, either by making promises to yourself (and keeping them) or by using some of the many tools presented in this book.

If you had three three-check answers, you are slightly above average in your "do-it-now!" abilities.

If you had four or five three-check answers, you are quite accomplished in your ability to overcome inertia and get things done.

Week 5:
Set deadlines.

African proverb: "Little by little, the cotton thread becomes a loincloth."

Experts tell us that the most efficient time managers spend a great deal of time each day on pressing issues but also spend a little time on issues with long-term deadlines. You should spend the lion's share of your day, about six hours altogether, on projects that need to be completed within the next six days. Allocate the remainder to projects with deadlines within the next six months.

If you haven't already divided your workload into these two broad divisions, take a moment to do so now. Don't procrastinate with this one: establish these deadlines so tomorrow you can work with your "6-hours/6-days/6-months" guideline.

Action Questions

1. What major projects do you face over the next six months?

_____

_____

_____

_____

2. What are you doing or have you done to move each of those along?

_____

_____

_____

_____

_____

_____

_____

_____

3. How are you keeping track of your progress on each project?

_____

_____

_____

_____

_____

_____

_____

Do It Now!

Set up folders for each of the major projects you must complete within the next six months. Write the name of the project and the deadline date on the outside of the folder in big, dark letters and numbers. It may be a good idea to identify the specific tasks you need to do to finish the project. Write these down on a sheet of paper and assign them completion dates. These are your project's mini-deadlines. Staple this sheet to the inside of your folder to track your progress.

Week 6:
Work for ten minutes.

Don Marquis: "Procrastination is the art of keeping up with yesterday."

No matter how repugnant the task, no matter how loathe you are to begin it, do it for just ten minutes. Set a timer and get to work, assuring yourself that you can tolerate the task for at least ten minutes.

When the timer goes off, ask yourself, "Can I stand it for another ten?" In all likelihood, you'll be so much "into it" that you won't mind continuing.

Action Questions

1. Do you regard yourself as "action-oriented"? Why or why not?

_____

_____

_____

_____

_____

2. Would you say your immediate boss is "action-oriented"? Describe his or her style.

_____

_____

_____

_____

_____

3. How well does your approach to work mesh with your boss's approach?

_____

_____

_____

_____

_____

Do It Now!

The word *procrastinate* literally means "for tomorrow" (from the Latin *pro* = for; *cras* = tomorrow). When you put things off for another day, you "procrastinate" by relegating duties from the present to the future. One quick visualization technique, designed to get you to do what should be done now, employs the "Pro-Hodie" button.

Whenever you are tempted to put something off "for tomorrow," pull into your mind the image of yourself wearing a Pro-Hodie (Latin, meaning "for today") badge like the one below. Sometimes the little nags are enough to force you to do what you must.

Week 7:
Reward yourself.

Anonymous: "Procrastination is a hardening of the oughteries."

Mind games have been played to keep people from insanity, boredom, and grief. Prisoners of war, for example, invent new alphabets or secret codes in order to face difficult circumstances without succumbing to them.

Fortunately, you can use mind games in circumstances that are far less serious. Whenever you work on something that you're tempted to postpone until tomorrow, reward yourself. Give yourself pep talks like the following:

- "If you can just file one inch off the stack, then you can go outside for a breath of fresh air."

- "Just do one more page of the report. Then you can get a cup of tea."

Action Questions

1. What brings you joy?

_____

_____

_____

_____

_____

_____

2. Which of these sources of joy could you tap as a reward for accomplishing tasks?

_____

_____

_____

_____

_____

_____

Do It Now!

Think about the ways you can reward yourself for doing work in the present instead of the future. List them here. Then the next time you do a task that you've been procrastinating or would like to procrastinate, choose a "treat" from the list and check it off.

☐ _____

☐ _____

☐ _____

☐ _____

☐ _____

☐ _____

☐ _____

☐ _____

☐ _____

Week 8:
Mentally prepare.

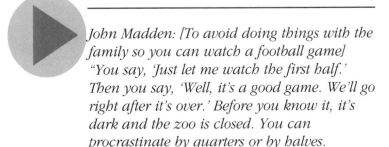

John Madden: [To avoid doing things with the family so you can watch a football game] "You say, 'Just let me watch the first half.' Then you say, 'Well, it's a good game. We'll go right after it's over.' Before you know it, it's dark and the zoo is closed. You can procrastinate by quarters or by halves. Procrastinating by halves is better."

Self-talk often leads to self-starts. When you can "psyche" yourself up for work to be done, you will probably find it is easier to begin the process that leads to fulfillment. When you self-talk, you set yourself up, quite literally, to tackle the less pleasant aspects of the project or assignment.

Self-talk is the best way to mentally prepare for assignments that call to you "Do me now!" The preparation is a prelude to delving into the seemingly insurmountable. There are several aspects to the preparation, which you will see depicted in the Mental Preparedness Wheel in the Do It Now exercise.

Action Questions

1. To what degree do you possess mental discipline?

_____

_____

_____

_____

2. What steps are involved in mentally preparing yourself for tasks that beckon you to procrastinate?

_____

_____

_____

_____

_____

_____

_____

Do It Now!

Look at the wheel of Mental Preparedness. With a bright color (preferably neon), circle the areas you need to develop further to maximize your receptiveness to accomplishing tedious tasks.

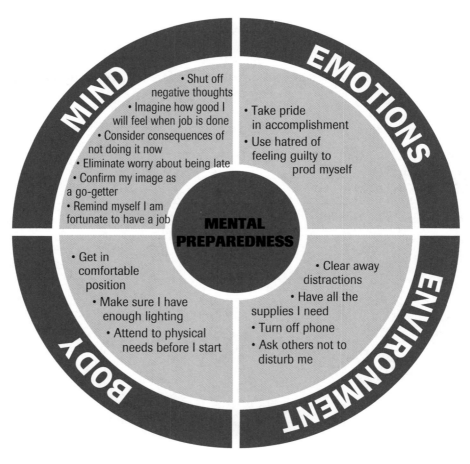

MIND
- Shut off negative thoughts
- Imagine how good I will feel when job is done
- Consider consequences of not doing it now
- Eliminate worry about being late
- Confirm my image as a go-getter
- Remind myself I am fortunate to have a job

EMOTIONS
- Take pride in accomplishment
- Use hatred of feeling guilty to prod myself

MENTAL PREPAREDNESS

BODY
- Get in comfortable position
- Make sure I have enough lighting
- Attend to physical needs before I start

ENVIRONMENT
- Clear away distractions
- Have all the supplies I need
- Turn off phone
- Ask others not to disturb me

Week 9:
Create the right atmosphere.

Henry G. Bohn: "One of these days is none of these days."

"Neat" does not necessarily mean efficient. Your office may resemble a junkyard, and yet you can immediately locate the files you need or the numbers you want. It is only when your system no longer serves you that you need to reorganize to a system that better suits you.

Elements of the "right" atmosphere may include motivational sayings or artwork on the wall, reminders of the vacation you can take as soon as you have completed the next major project, an extensive filing system or an understanding with friends, family, and co-workers that when you do not want to be disturbed, you do not want to be disturbed.

Action Questions

1. What factors in your environment influence you to work steadily instead of postponing?

   _____

   _____

   _____

   _____

2. Which factors tend to distract you or encourage procrastination?

   _____

   _____

   _____

   _____

3. What can you do to eliminate or lessen the power of the procrastination forces that surround you?

   _____

   _____

   _____

   _____

Do It Now!

Using the following scale, evaluate yourself on each of the following statements.

1 = Not able and not willing

2 = Able but not willing

3 = Not able but willing

4 = Able *and* willing

1. _____ Create work space that is conducive to getting work done

2. _____ Tell others that I cannot be disturbed for certain periods

3. _____ Have visible reminders of how important it is to be on top of things

4. _____ Create a filing system that allows me to find things instantly

5. _____ Have *both* an "open-door" and a "closed-door" policy

Immediately implement the actions you rated as "4."

For the answers you gave as "1," "2," or "3," record here exactly why you are not able and/or not willing to perform certain actions that will enhance your work environment.

_____

_____

_____

_____

_____

_____

_____

_____

_____

Can you do anything to convert your unwillingness to acceptance?

_____

_____

_____

_____

_____

_____

Week 10:
Allocate minutes for distant projects.

Edward Young: "Procrastination is the thief of time."

Deadlines have a way of creeping up quietly and then bludgeoning you with their urgency. While some people purport to work best when their "backs are up against the wall," most people are uncomfortable in this position and often find they make mistakes when the metaphoric "pushes" become "shoves."

One way to overcome deadline disasters is to begin working on faraway projects long before the due date. Check with your boss to find out what he or she needs or wants you to do within the next year—beyond what you find in your job description.

List those long-range projects, ones that do not require your immediate attention, on the form provided in the Do It Now! exercise.

Action Questions

1. Are you one of those people who "works well under pressure"? Explain.

_____

_____

_____

_____

_____

_____

2. How can you be sure you wouldn't work even better if the pressure were removed?

_____

_____

_____

_____

_____

Do It Now!

List here the projects that you and your boss want to accomplish within the next year.

Then predict how many minutes you think you can steal from other work this week to spend on these projects. Write those numbers in the second column.

Finally, as you carve out minutes this week, tally them and see how closely your actual time matches your prediction. Keep the tally going every week until the projects are completed. As you extend this exercise, you'll find your estimates becoming more accurate and your time management skills increasing.

Long-Range Projects and Due Dates	This week, I estimate I can spend:	This week, I actually spent:
1. _____	_____	_____
2. _____	_____	_____
3. _____	_____	_____
4. _____	_____	_____
5. _____	_____	_____

Comments from Richard P. Ciminelli, an expert on procrastination and assistant director of the Management Development Center, United States Office of Personnel Management

I have pondered the meaning of "procrastination" for years. (It has caused me much lost sleep.) There's always tomorrow, or so it seems. Who are procrastinators? They are a blend of both healthy and unhealthy dimensions.

On the healthy side, procrastination slows one down from what could be rash, impetuous actions that one may later regret (and have to pay for). On the negative side, procrastination leads to disorganized thinking and a form of behavioral paralysis that can cause major losses.

I have almost always stalled for more time and greater options. Over the years, this stalling has generally worked to my advantage. In fact, I am so good at it that if I rush out full of plans and make quick decisions, things usually don't fall into place.

I will admit, though, that some procrastinators may be avoiding necessary action … action that may be personally painful. We all have engaged in avoidance behavior at one time or another. For most of us, fortunately, it's not a repetitive behavioral pattern. For those who do have this pattern, though, the cure is more arduous than doing the work we avoided.

Let me deal with the healthy procrastinator, the person like me who postpones wisely. This sort of person seldom needs input. However, skilled people can adroitly provide constructive feedback at appropriate times. This means active listening skills, positive self-reinforcement, no personal attacks, a tone that is friendly, patience, and a coaching mentality. Specifics really help.

For example, I have some work schedule deadlines that are initially self-selected. Once set, they cannot be changed. Things will happen even if I am not there. This allows me to channel my attention and behavior toward specific work targets. Consequences are critical. Being aware of all this, I choose my procrastination targets wisely. But if I am not hitting the targets, I may elicit or receive some constructive feedback.

For the unwise procrastinator, a harsh and demanding approach is sometimes used. And, it does get some short-term results. Most often, however, it yields passive-aggressive behavior and possibly even a permanently damaged relationship. In the work environment, this deteriorated relationship can spell long-term trouble.

A foundation built on inspiration helps both the healthy and the unhealthy procrastinator realize that perspiration is worthwhile. For those of you wanting to help procrastinators become more productive, follow these steps for building the inspiration-foundation:

- **Set** goals with the procrastinator.
- **Identify** the important ends.
- **Assess** the procrastinator's progress.
- **Offer** feedback to the procrastinator.
- **Make** changes in goals or level of progress if necessary.
- **Give** rewards for accomplishment.
- **Have** procrastinators assist one another.

Week 11:
Use spare moments to make notes about your plan of attack.

Norman Cousins: "Progress begins with the belief that what is necessary is possible."

Everyone wastes moments each day—some are self-imposed but others we have little control over—traffic tie-ups, for example, or long lines in banks, or being put on hold on the telephone.

The good news is that we have control over our reactions. Instead of becoming frustrated, we can choose to use the time well and, in so doing, lessen the stress involved. And, choosing to be more productive in the present can save time later.

Here's a real-life example: An author promised himself he would outline a book on a recent flight. Being an author he naturally loved to read and became so absorbed in a book that he forgot about his intentions until he heard the pilot announce, "We will be landing in Pittsburgh in twenty minutes." Startled into activity, he used those twenty minutes to outline the upcoming book's chapters. The outline became reality a year later when the book was published.

He could have looked out the window, chatted with a fellow passenger, glanced through a magazine, cat-napped, or continued with his book. Instead, he used the remaining time to plan his next project.

Planning, even if it's only making a rough sketch of how you'll proceed or a numbered list of what needs to be done, is an excellent prod. When you know what you will do and how you'll do it, the actual physical act is less of a burden.

Action Questions

1. How do you keep track of the good but random thoughts that drift into your mind concerning work responsibilities (how and when do you record them, for example)?

_____

_____

_____

_____

2. How do others in your environment manage to keep mentally organized?

_____

_____

_____

_____

3. Do you honestly believe that using spare minutes can help shape future projects? Explain why or why not.

_____

_____

_____

_____

_____

Do It Now!

Place an "X" in the box that most closely represents your planning style.

1. How much planning do you do?

   None—until it's time to begin the project. □ □ □ □ □ I think it through well in advance.

   1 2 3 4 5

2. How much time do you waste in a day?

   I don't accomplish much unless I can block out chunks of time. □ □ □ □ □ I'm a time-miser: I don't waste any time at all.

   1 2 3 4 5

3. How flexible are you when it comes to planning?

   I can't think unless I have a keyboard in front of me. □ □ □ □ □ Just give me a pencil and a sheet of paper—I'll be fine.

   1 2 3 4 5

4. How well/quickly do you write?

   I write slowly because I'm a terrible speller. □ □ □ □ □ I don't get hung up with correctness—I just want to get the thoughts down.

   1 2 3 4 5

5. How much socializing do you do in a typical day?

| Two to three hours a day, counting lunch, breaks, and normal friendly chats. | ☐ 1 | ☐ 2 | ☐ 3 | ☐ 4 | ☐ 5 | Beyond pleasantries, I avoid discussing anything that isn't work-related. |

Having completed the quiz, take stock of your answers. Are they telling you that you're as good as you can be, or are they suggesting a need for some improvement?

If the message you're getting is that you need improvement, confer with someone (at a level higher than your own, if possible) you regard as an excellent planner or strategist. Show that person your results and ask for advice. Implement that advice.

Then, come back to this exercise in one month. Reevaluate yourself to see if there is any improvement in the way you use spare moments to get projects under way.

Week 12:
Align your objectives with those of your boss.

Fanny Kemble: "Fail not for sorrow, falter not for sin; But onward, upward, till the goal ye win."

It's been said that what you cannot communicate can ruin your life. If your priorities differ from those of your boss, the two of you will be working against each other. Clarifying objectives benefits you in a number of ways:

- It makes others aware of your desire to be efficient.

- Once common goals have been established, it will be harder for you to procrastinate. Your boss will now be involved in your progress.

- While you work on those jobs that are most relevant to the organizational mission (and, consequently, relegate tasks of lesser importance to lesser positions on your hierarchy of responsibilities), you will save time.

- It furthers the sense of partnership between you and your boss.

- It paves the way for further dialogues about the work before you.

The meeting you hold to clarify objectives between the two of you need not be a long one. But it *is* important. Not only does it confirm that you are making the best possible use of your time, but it will work in your favor when your boss reviews your performance.

Action Questions

1. When was the last time you and your boss sat down to discuss objectives? What happened? Describe the circumstances.

2. What can you do to improve the type and frequency of communications with your boss?

Do It Now!

Select one of the following drawings that most closely resembles the degree of alignment (about work projects) that currently exists between you and your boss.

A	B	C	D	E

Explain here which drawing you chose and why.

_____

_____

_____

_____

_____

_____

_____

_____

_____

_____

Now, ask your boss to complete the same exercise (another set of questions is provided on the next page). Once he or she has written out an explanation, compare your responses.

Do It Now! (For Your Boss)

Select one of the following drawings that most closely resembles the degree of alignment (about work projects) that currently exists between you and your associate.

A   B   C   D   E

Explain here which drawing you chose and why.

_____

_____

_____

_____

_____

_____

_____

_____

_____

_____

_____

_____

_____

_____

Week 13:
Use the "poke-holes" approach.

Edmund Burke: "Nobody makes a greater mistake than he who did nothing because he could only do a little."

Since the ancient Romans articulated their *divida et vinca* ("divide and conquer") approach to geographic and cultural aggrandizement, a number of experts have applied the philosophy to the management of time. Sometimes called the "Swiss cheese" method or the "salami" technique, this weapon could prove to be especially useful in your time management efforts. Rather than feeling overwhelmed by the enormity of a given task, simply find ways in which you can successfully conquer some of the components of the task.

If, for example, you have to write a booklet detailing the evacuation procedures to be followed in the event of a fire, the "holes" you need to poke might be making phone calls to the fire captain and other organizations that have already prepared their safety procedures. Another "hole" might be to start a folder with articles concerning fire safety. Another might be dividing the broad topic into several subtopics or putting the outline into a computer file.

Action Questions

1. Choose a large project that's facing you and briefly describe it here.

   _____

   _____

   _____

2. How can you use the "poke-holes" approach to tackle the assignment a bit at a time?

   _____

   _____

   _____

   _____

3. What sequential steps will you follow?

   _____

   _____

   _____

   _____

   _____

   _____

   _____

   _____

Do It Now!

Answer these "extent" question by placing an "X" in the appropriate box. If your response is "to a large extent," place a star (a large one, even a gold one) in the box instead of an "X."

To what extent do you:

1. Admit the importance of getting started?

   ☐   ☐   ☐
   To no extent   To some extent   To a large extent

2. Feel gratified by small advances?

   ☐   ☐   ☐
   To no extent   To some extent   To a large extent

3. Believe in the "divide and conquer" philosophy?

   ☐   ☐   ☐
   To no extent   To some extent   To a large extent

4. Remind yourself of past successes?

   ☐   ☐   ☐
   To no extent   To some extent   To a large extent

5. Acknowledge the importance of short-term goals?

   ☐   ☐   ☐
   To no extent   To some extent   To a large extent

Week 14:
Clear away the "fluff."

Mae West: "He who hesitates is last."

Accommodate your idiosyncrasies! If you're one of those people who doesn't feel comfortable delving into a long-term project until you can clear away smaller obligations, fine! Just make certain you allow yourself only a certain amount of time for fluff-clearing. Otherwise, it will consume the entire morning (or even the entire day) and you will be left wondering where time went.

Small tasks are important—that can't be denied. You can start with them or start with the big tasks—it doesn't matter. Just roll up your sleeves and make some headway. But set an alarm clock first. When it goes off, say at 10:30 in the morning, stop your work on the large project and spend some time on those small (but significant) obligations. Or vice versa.

A third possibility is to divide the major project into stopping points. When you reach such a point, take a break by handling one of the "fluff" jobs. Or vise versa.

Action Questions

1. How do you typically deal with the small jobs you must do each day?

   _____

   _____

   _____

   _____

   _____

   _____

2. Have you ever ignored them so you could make serious progress on an extended assignment? If so, what were the consequences? If not, what drives you to get rid of the daily fluff so conscientiously?

   _____

   _____

   _____

   _____

   _____

   _____

Do It Now!

Here's something simple that will help you make the transition to and from the major and minor tasks:

> Place a finger as hard as you can in the slight hollow that appears beneath your nostrils and above the center of your upper lip.

For some reason, the pressure that is exerted quickens our thinking about, and heightens our awareness of, the work to be done. It even works when you find yourself nodding off in meetings or when you feel sleepy while driving a car.

Week 15:
Delegate or relegate dislikes.

Danish proverb: "A man cannot whistle and drink at the same time."

Delegation, when handled properly, yields win/win outcomes. You can delegate, after thoughtful discussion with an associate, tasks you don't especially enjoy but another person does.

Decide if you would prefer to "whistle" or to "drink." And then find someone who will take over the tasks you dislike. One caveat: Don't just *dump* the tasks you dislike on someone else who finds no pleasure in doing them. Make sure the person you delegate them to finds them meaningful.

Action Questions

1. Think about which jobs you dislike. What common elements do they share?

   _____

   _____

   _____

   _____

2. Do the same for your preferred tasks. What is it about the nature of these tasks that you enjoy?

   _____

   _____

   _____

   _____

3. Other than delegating, how can you reduce the number of tasks you dislike and increase the number of (or the time you can spend on) tasks you prefer?

   _____

   _____

   _____

   _____

Do It Now!

In the first column on the next page, list five tasks you can delegate.

In the second column, rank each task in terms of how much you dislike doing it, using the measures that follow.

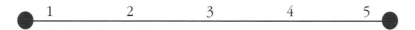

I like it no more, no less than my other tasks.

I do it, but my heart's not really in it.

I hate doing this so much that it sometimes makes me physically ill.

In the third column, write the name of a person to whom you might delegate the job. Find out how the person feels about this particular job and write a number to reflect his or her enjoyment of it, using this scale.

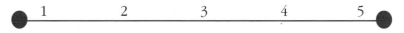

He or she gets physically ill, just thinking about it.

He or she would trade it if it were possible.

He or she loves doing this kind of work.

Finally, in the fourth column, write a number to indicate the likelihood of success should this delegation become reality. The number will be the result of multiplying the numbers in the second column (your degree of dislike) and the third column (the other person's degree of like for the task).

Task to delegate	How much do you dislike it? (1 to 5)	Who might like it and how much? (1 to 5)	What is the likelihood of success?
1. _____	_____	_____	_____
2. _____	_____	_____	_____
3. _____	_____	_____	_____
4. _____	_____	_____	_____
5. _____	_____	_____	_____

Those tasks with a final score of 20 or more are excellent candidates for delegation. Pursue the possibilities further.

Week 16:
Regard the unappealing task as a challenge.

Sophocles: "The immortal gods alone have neither age nor death! All other things almighty Time disquiets."

Nietzsche knew that what "does not kill us makes us stronger." Your "must-do" tasks certainly are not toxic. Unpleasant, perhaps, but not poisonous. By confronting your reluctance, by proving you are stronger than the forces urging you to put things off for yet another day, you will emerge victorious on more levels than one.

Tell yourself you will postpone unappealing tasks no longer. Meet the challenge and meet a stronger you in the process.

Action Questions

1. What kinds of tasks do you regard as personal challenges?

   _____

   _____

   _____

   _____

   _____

2. How exactly *do* these tasks challenge you?

   _____

   _____

   _____

   _____

   _____

3. Are you competitive? to what degree?

   _____

   _____

   _____

   _____

   _____

Do It Now!

Reproduce the following graphic and distribute it to eight or ten trusted colleagues. Ask each to anonymously write your name in the area that most typifies your ability to defeat procrastination. Then, have them mail you the assessment or leave it on your desk when you're not around.

If you repeatedly see your name on the right-hand side of the graphic, you can sleep easily. However, if (in the estimation of your colleagues) you tend to put off until tomorrow what really should be done today, you may wish to set a goal of acquiring as habits many of the procrastination-busting recommendations in this book.

Sometimes, learning what others think about our behaviors goads us into action. If you *are* a procrastinator, having your colleagues point it out to you may be enough to help you change your ways.

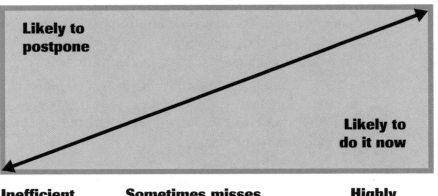

Week 17:
Slip a task you dislike between favorite ones.

Ecclesiastes: "Time and chance happeneth to them all."

Those we admire for their discipline have learned what works for them in defeating procrastination. Talk to a dozen different disciplined individuals and you will probably hear a dozen different techniques. Some use visualization; others a reward system. Some prefer self-talk, while others depend on coaches or friends. This book gives you a wide array of possibilities to choose from as you develop your discipline regime. This week's weapon is an easy one to practice and a good one for producing results.

Indulge yourself. Go ahead. Do the things you most like to do. But for every one hour you spend on a favored chore, spend fifteen minutes on one you dislike. It really is the old carrot-on-a-stick routine, used in reverse.

Action Questions

1. Remember yourself as a child (or think about your own children or grandchildren). What sort of thing energized you? What kind of task did you need no external prompting to complete?

   _____

   _____

   _____

   _____

2. Think creatively. How could you bring that enthusiasm to the tasks you typically procrastinate?

   _____

   _____

   _____

   _____

3. Going one step further, could some of those driving forces work on an organizational level?

   _____

   _____

   _____

   _____

Do It Now!

For each technique, place a check mark in the appropriate box on the left to indicate how important the technique is in helping you defeat procrastination and another check mark in the box on the right to indicate how frequently you use this technique.

How Important
Is It To Do This?

How Often Do I
Do This?

Not at all	Some- what	Very		Never	Some- times	Always
☐	☐	☐	1. I play tricks on myself in order to stay motivated.	☐	☐	☐
☐	☐	☐	2. I can talk myself into a positive mind-set.	☐	☐	☐
☐	☐	☐	3. I need to relieve the tedium of some work.	☐	☐	☐
☐	☐	☐	4. I try not to get fatigued, helping to avoid errors.	☐	☐	☐
☐	☐	☐	5. I stick with a plan I've established.	☐	☐	☐

There are no real right or wrong answers here. Instead, the quiz should afford you some insight into your willingness to try some new weapons in the war against procrastination and to learn more about yourself.

The more you think positively about your capacity to do work when it's before you, the more successful you will be in your antiprocrastination efforts. Relieving tedium (and being creative enough to find the ways you can) is important as you seek to reduce stress and bring joy back to the work you do. Tedium leads to tiredness, which in turn leads to errors. The best plan for you is a plan of your own devising. You know your own biorhythms and when they can be put to best use. You know when you tend to experience burnout, when you need refreshment, and when you must switch the pace or the place or the work itself.

Try out various plans that mix tedious tasks with your favorite ones. Stick with each plan for at least a week so you can get a true feel for the one that works best for you.

Week 18:
Find a buddy who's willing to check up on you.

Leo Tolstoi: "The strongest of all warriors are these two—Time and Patience."

In societies and organizations, no one functions independently. An insular life may work for the few true "loners" who exist outside community confines, but within the workplace we depend on one another. Finding a buddy to help you defeat the procrastination foe may be one of the smartest things you can do.

Strange as it may seem, it may be best to seek someone who suffers from the same malady. This way, you can serve as mutual motivators.

Action Questions

1. Who is a good candidate for serving as a fellow soldier in the war against procrastination?

   _____

   _____

   _____

2. What exactly would you like your buddy to do?

   _____

   _____

   _____

   _____

3. At what point will you no longer need that person's services? What criteria will you set for yourself?

   _____

   _____

   _____

   _____

   _____

Do It Now!

1. For each item, use an "X" to mark the spot where you are now and an "O" to mark where you would like to be.

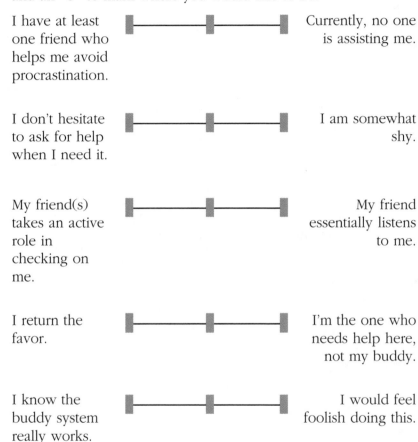

I have at least one friend who helps me avoid procrastination.
⊢————⊣————⊣
Currently, no one is assisting me.

I don't hesitate to ask for help when I need it.
⊢————⊣————⊣
I am somewhat shy.

My friend(s) takes an active role in checking on me.
⊢————⊣————⊣
My friend essentially listens to me.

I return the favor.
⊢————⊣————⊣
I'm the one who needs help here, not my buddy.

I know the buddy system really works.
⊢————⊣————⊣
I would feel foolish doing this.

2. Now look over the spots where you placed "X" and "O" marks. Which item has the biggest gap between your "X" and "O" marks?

_____

_____

_____

_____

3. What can you do to reduce that gap?

_____

_____

_____

_____

Week 19:
Energize yourself.

Albert de la Martine: "Let us savor the fleeting delights of our most beautiful days!"

Just as corporations understand the importance of occasionally shifting paradigms, so must we as individuals be willing to adapt to new mind-sets in order to produce better results. Reminding yourself of the delights interspersed with the tedium of your days contributes to a positive mind-set and has an energizing effect.

It is possible to talk yourself into something. Try doing something physical first (or last), getting a snack, reading something inspirational, or playing a tape recording of the boss stressing the importance of a deadline. It doesn't matter what you select to take your mind out of the doldrums and into the dynamism of achievement. But, by this stage in your life, you should have discovered someone or something that energizes you and stimulates you to act.

Action Questions

1. Think about yourself in your most energetic state. What makes you that way? Describe yourself and the energizing conditions.

_____

_____

_____

_____

_____

2. To what extent is it difficult for you to talk yourself out of a bad mood or lethargic frame of mind? Explain.

_____

_____

_____

_____

_____

_____

_____

Do It Now!

Keep adding to this list of energy boosters that are good for you. (Have your friends contribute ideas too.) Use as many as you need each day. Check them off as you go to prevent yourself from becoming dependent on any particular one. Variety, after all, is the spice of life.

_____	Eating fresh fruit
_____	Drinking sparkling water
_____	Calling a colleague or customer you really like
_____	Washing your face
_____	Getting a cup of coffee or tea
_____	Walking up a flight of stairs
_____	Reading a few jokes from a joke book
_____	Working on a puzzle for a few minutes
_____	Reading a poem
_____	Looking at a travel brochure
_____	Snacking on nonfat yogurt
_____	Playing with the dog

_____ _____

_____ _____

_____ _____

_____ _____

_____ _____

_____ _____

Week 20:
Develop your powers of concentration.

Henry Wadsworth Longfellow: "Time is fleeting."

Some people pride themselves on being able to do many things at once. Even if this were possible, it would probably mean many things were being done *poorly* at once and without the concentration the task at hand requires.

No matter what your current potential for concentration is, you can always make it better. One aid is to make the environment as conducive as possible for the heady work you have to do. Another is to parcel out the work in time segments that are manageable for you. Another is to have all the tools for the challenging assignment ready and in place.

Action Questions

1. No one knows you the way *you* know you. When are your powers of concentration most intense?

   _____

   _____

   _____

   _____

   _____

2. How hard is it (or will it be) for you to replicate the conditions under which you work at peak proficiency?

   _____

   _____

   _____

   _____

   _____

Do It Now!

Cluster the tasks you are prone to postpone into groups of five. As you complete each cluster, do the following energizing activity (which is also designed to improve your powers of concentration and your memory): Ask a friend to read you a four-digit number. Then repeat it—*backwards*.

When you have completed the next five-item bundle, ask the same friend to read you the same number if you were not correct in your backwards-recall, or a new number if you were successful. This time, the new number should have *five* digits.

This activity provides a good break, as it requires intense concentration—you must stop thinking about one thing and concentrate on another. It also provides fun without wasting time. (If you do this twelve times a day, you and your friend will spend a total of less than two minutes.) Each time you're successful with your backwards-recall, elevate yourself to the next level, a number one digit longer than the previous one. Believe it or not, you can develop your skills to the point at which you can repeat backwards a twelve- or fifteen-digit number.

When you reach this stage, reward yourself!

Interview with Maria Ciaccia

Maria Ciaccia is head writer for *The World Times* and author of *Bloomin', Dreamboats: Hollywood Hunks of the '50s* and *Complete Preparation: A Guide to Auditioning for Opera* (with Joan Dornemann). She is also a research assistant for Barry Paris, author of biographies on Greta Garbo, Audrey Hepburn, and Louise Brooks.

The procrastination dragon? Sure, I know how to defeat him. Let me count the ways for you.

- *Slay the overwhelm dragon.* When I look at a big project or a mountain of work, it's tough to get started. Breaking a task down into parts is a good way to begin.

  I also think long-term so that I can complete a project in bite-sized chunks, rather than wait until the day before it's due. I work on one element of an assignment each day. However, I impose a deadline date by which the entire job needs to be done.

- *Planned procrastination.* I set time aside for procrastination-type activities weekly. I take a morning for paying bills, writing letters, getting things ready to mail, copying, or sending faxes, for instance. Also, as a freelancer who makes her own schedule, I put aside time for running errands like taking in the cleaning, doing the laundry, taking out the garbage, or going to the bank, to the post office, or shopping.

- *Don't begin at the beginning.* The beginning of a project can often be the most daunting part. It sometimes helps to start in the middle—a writing project is a good case in point. The beginning is the hardest part. Doing some of the middle section or writing the end often inspires me for the beginning.

- *Time, thou glittering bauble.* For freelancers like me, the difficult thing is to keep time from getting away. I find that scheduling something in my date book helps me to commit to that "promise-on-paper." For instance, writing "catch up" in my book on a certain morning helps me schedule things around that section.

- *Don't procrastinate.* One key to avoiding procrastination is to just do the thing immediately when it's in front of you, like returning the phone call or sorting the mail or writing the letter. Handling it at the moment keeps it from becoming a task I can procrastinate.

- *Time well-spent.* A key reason for procrastination is not being able to find the time. So I've learned to use my time well. Watching television, for example, is a prime opportunity to do things like addressing envelopes; traveling on public transportation is a great time to catch up on reading.

- *Promise her anything.* Behavior modification is another tool. "Do this thing for one hour and then you can watch your soap opera." I talk to myself the way I would talk to a recalcitrant child.

I also follow some famous dictums from the theater in order to overcome procrastination:

- *"To thine own self be true." [Hamlet]* I know my own clock. In the morning, I'm freshest for mental activities like writing. Around noon is best for running errands and going to the health club. The afternoon is a good time to schedule interviews for my newspaper.

For something you tend to put off, your most alert time or most unencumbered time (i.e., free of phone or visitor interruptions) is best. This is usually early morning.

- *"The kindness of strangers."* *[A Streetcar Named Desire]* It's often a good idea to ask for help. A friend coming over on a Saturday afternoon to help with a mailing or with a closet-clean-out, a group helping to put a project together—these are things to look forward to, not put off. Afterwards, buy lunch or treat everyone to a movie.

- *"Money, money, money."* *[Cabaret]* Jack Nicholson once said people are unwilling to solve problems by spending money. If you procrastinate about cleaning your house, your ironing, or your errand-running, can you afford to have someone do it for you? Think creatively. Many of us have out-of-work friends.

- *"Double, double, toil and trouble."* *[MacBeth]* I always keep this in mind: if I procrastinate, it just means there will be double to do tomorrow.

Week 21:
Remind yourself of the consequences.

Herman Hupfeld: "The fundamental things apply, as time goes by."

You probably know several people who are their own worst enemies. Conversely, it's possible for you to be your own best friend. Just as good friends can help talk you out of bad decisions (or can at least listen as you try to talk yourself out of or into them), you can use inner resources to help you face the work today rather than the worries tomorrow.

Remind yourself of the consequences of not finishing the task right now. Contemplating the problems likely to ensue from missed deadlines shakes most people into action. (On the other hand, if the consequences aren't dire, it may be best to procrastinate, especially if fatigue has pushed you to the point of diminishing returns.)

Action Questions

1. Think of a time when you resisted the urge to procrastinate and were glad you did.

   _____

   _____

   _____

   _____

2. Knowing your boss as you do, what consequences does he or she have in store for people who procrastinate repeatedly?

   _____

   _____

   _____

   _____

3. Do you feel comfortable making excuses when you miss deadlines because you've procrastinated? If not, let that uneasiness jolt you into action to complete the task you keep postponing.

   _____

   _____

   _____

Do It Now!

The next time you're tempted to let the procrastination monster defeat you, take a few moments to stare at this wheel and mentally turn it using only "yes" answers to move to the next position. If you can still answer "yes" when you get to the sixth position, then go ahead and procrastinate. At least you will be doing so having carefully weighed the consequences.

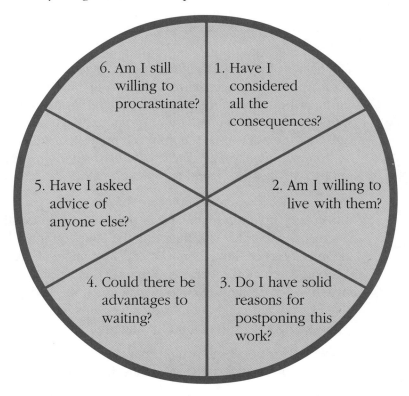

Note: The fifth question isn't as pertinent to trivial tasks as it is to the ones that really matter. Asking someone to help you evaluate the consequences of your procrastination could be a crucial factor in your decision to do or put off the task.

Week 22:
Keep a "tickler" file.

Lord Chesterfield: "The less one has to do, the less time one finds to do it."

The tickler file is a weapon that yields mighty results with minimal effort from you. To get started, simply purchase a box with cardboard divisions for the twelve months (available in most office supply stores). Each time you're given an assignment, slip a dated card into the appropriate month to remind yourself of what needs to be done and when. The date on the card should be several days prior to the task's required completion date.

For example, if you're responsible for organizing the office Christmas party, you might slip into the November section a card dated November 12. This might be the date you intend to send out the invitations or the announcement. You might slip in another card, this one dated November 1, to remind you to purchase the invitations or design the announcements. If the invitations are to be mailed, you will need another card, perhaps dated November 9, reminding you to spend the morning addressing the invitations.

In December, you'll insert more new cards to remind you about other responsibilities associated with the party.

Each morning, you'll open up your tickler file to see what's in store for that day. It will "tickle" you to see how efficient this simple tool can make you.

Action Questions

1. What's the likelihood you'll actually use the tickler file once you've set it up?

   _____

   _____

   _____

2. If you think you'll forget to use it or if the system just doesn't suit your style, what comparable system could you employ (electronic, perhaps?) to remind you of project deadlines?

   _____

   _____

   _____

   _____

   _____

Do It Now!

To illustrate the importance of being organized—with tickler files or any other method that works well for you—imagine you've been asked to learn a new code. The same information appears in both columns below but is organized differently. Which column do you think would help you to more efficiently absorb the information you need to learn?

Column A

1	2	3	4
5	6	7	8
9	10		

Column B

10	9	5
8	7	2
6	3	4
	1	

In Column A, you see an orderly progression right away. The tickler file, in a sense, functions in the same way. You already know what you have to do. But if the knowledge is scattered haphazardly around your desk, within your computer, or throughout your various work spaces (as in Column B), you'll have a hard time assimilating the information and getting an accurate sense of the big picture.

Week 23:
Keep a diary of your successes.

William James: "Nothing is so fatiguing as the eternal hanging of an uncompleted task."

Each of us can benefit from keeping a diary of successes.

You don't need to write in your diary daily, and the entries don't need to be lengthy. You don't have to share it with anyone. But each time you're successful in forcing yourself to move forward, even when every nerve ending in your body is screaming "Enough!" make a note detailing your state of mind or the external person or thing that inspired you to move on instead of out. The Action Questions may help you get started.

Action Questions

1. What specific thoughts are useful in propelling you forward?

_____

_____

_____

_____

_____

2. How do you reward yourself for sticking with a difficult project longer than you wanted to?

_____

_____

_____

_____

_____

Do It Now!

Imagine the "critical path" that will lead you to both immediate and long-range career success. In the graphic below, begin by defining your destination (one of your goals), and then list the obstacles to reaching it. Also list the activities that will help you achieve it. Anticipating the obstacles gives you the opportunity to find ways to overcome them or avoid them altogether instead of letting them become a source of procrastination.

What is your "destination"?

_____

Which obstacles are likely to sidetrack you?

Which activities will take you there?

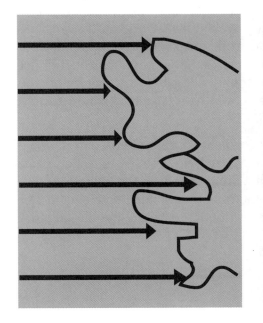

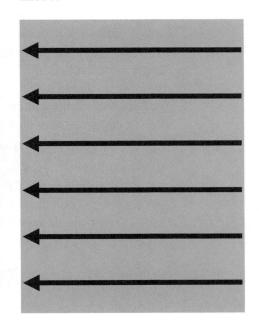

Week 24:
Relegate disruptions to a list.

Napoleon Bonaparte: "You can ask me for anything you like, except time."

More often than not, you can simply make a note of what needs to be done instead of getting up to respond immediately to needs that arise. Let's say you begin to work and discover your favorite pen is missing. Use a pencil for now and make a note to look for the pen later. As you're working, the boss calls for the variance report from last month. Ask if you can take it to him this afternoon. If so, make a note to do so and get back to work. Your next interruption is your most important client, who wants to set up an appointment. Tell her you need to check your calendar and will get back to her before the day is over. Then make a note of what you have to do and return to the begging-to-be-postponed task.

Once you have completed the segment you promised yourself you'd get done today, then you can play catch-up with the things on your list. By the way, if your personal prime time is in the afternoon, set an alarm to go off forty-five minutes before quitting time so you can take care of the items on your disruption list before the business day ends.

Action Questions

1. You can form new habits by practicing them over a two-week period. What would it take for you to form the "list-disruptions" habit? Here's one idea you can try: Consider some of the routine disruptions/interruptions you encounter every day. Write them down below. Identifying these disruptions now will make you more aware of them as disrupters the next time they occur. Instead of stopping what you're doing to take care of them, you'll recognize them as disrupters and be more inclined to simply make a note of them and take care of them later.

---

2. What explains the perseverance of the most time-efficient person you know?

Do It Now!

Here are five keys to help you put disruptions aside. Read the list aloud to yourself at the beginning of every day this week. If you know you'll be working on a task you especially dislike (and can therefore easily be distracted from), read the list again before beginning the actual task.

1. I'm disciplined enough to note all the people and things that may demand my time instead of stopping to respond to each call (unless of course it's an emergency situation).

2. I'm interested enough to examine the list at the end of each day (for at least a week) to learn what kinds of interruptions may be tempting me to procrastinate.

3. I'm tactful enough to advise co-workers (without alienating them) of the times when I can't be interrupted.

4. I'm realistic enough to know I'm capable of eliminating some of the distractions that currently plague me.

5. I'm professional enough to follow through on all the distractions I temporarily put aside in order to make a serious dent in a complicated project.

Week 25:
Nag yourself.

Thomas a Kempis: "Remember that lost time does not return."

Just as some executives pinch themselves in order to stay awake at dull meetings, many successful time "masters" mentally pinch themselves whenever they need that extra spurt to finish a tough assignment.

This technique involves self-talk, but self-talk with "an attitude," so to speak. This is no time for the endearments or courtesies of confidence-building. The nag in you should be abrasive, abrupt, and absorbed with a singular purpose: getting you across the goal line. You can use the Do It Now! exercise to spur yourself to action or, if you'd rather, compose a more menacing monologue.

Action Questions

1. In what other areas besides overcoming procrastination do you use self-talk to help you overcome difficult events or difficult people?

   _____

   _____

   _____

   _____

   _____

2. What specific benefits accrue to you because of these self-talks?

   _____

   _____

   _____

   What benefits can accrue from self-talk about procrastination?

   _____

   _____

   _____

3. Think of a person whose accomplishments you admire. What do you think his or her "nag-monologue" sounds like?

   _____

   _____

   _____

   _____

   _____

   _____

Do It Now!

Prepare a 3 x 5 card with the following statements. Then, when the Procrastination Monster begins to approach, pull out the card and use it to nag yourself into action.

> **I can** stand doing just a few minutes of this unlikable job.
>
> **I can** see the advantage to tackling this now. (Then mentally tick off the consequences of not doing it right way.)
>
> **I can** always quit when I reach the saturation point.
>
> **I can** boast to _____ afterwards about how good I am.
>
> **I can** make tomorrow easier by doing this today.

Week 26:
Let a master procrastinator be your anti-hero.

Bob Murphy: "The only person to succeed while horsing around is a bookie."

More than one management guru has noted that we live in an age of paradox. One paradox that applies to your anti-procrastination endeavors is this: You can learn good lessons from those who are poor examples.

Look around you. Find the worst procrastinator you know. Consider how procrastination has sabotaged his or her career. As an added incentive, ask your co-workers, in general terms, how they view people who procrastinate. Then determine that you will be the *opposite* of that person in terms of procrastinating behavior.

Action Questions

1. Do you think it's possible that some people cling to their procrastinating behavior because they think it's an unalterable part of their personality? Explain your answer.

_____

_____

_____

_____

_____

_____

2. What other lessons about time have you learned from people who do not use it well?

_____

_____

_____

_____

Do It Now!

Without naming names, think about the worst procrastinator you know. Now, list all the weaknesses this person exhibits and all the negative results that his or her procrastinating behavior produces.

_____

_____

_____

_____

_____

_____

_____

_____

_____

_____

_____

_____

_____

Now place an exclamation point [!] beside the traits that you also possess. From time to time, turn to this page and think about this person. Promise yourself not to be like him or her any longer. Commit to changing your ways so others will not view you as _you_ view the master procrastinator.

Work to eliminate, one at a time, the behaviors you marked with an exclamation point.

Week 27:
Let your biorhythms be your guide.

James T. McCay: "You can only manage time in those moments when you are alert to what is going on within you and around you."

Whether you're aware of it or not, the internal clock that ticks inside you forces you to make decisions about your life. One of the minor decisions you make is when you should handle the responsibilities that await you each day. If you haven't yet determined the best time for doing your most difficult tasks, start paying attention to the times during the day when you say to yourself, "I'm really getting a lot done!" Then, jot down what time of day it is and wait for a pattern to emerge.

Once you've determined when you operate at your greatest efficiency, use that time to do at least *some* of the tasks you'd like to put off for another day.

Action Questions

1. Chronobiologists and NLP (neurolinguistic programmers) advocates suggest we align our high-performance hours with the peak-performance periods of other people we work with. When does your boss seem to be operating at prime efficiency?

   _____

   _____

2. Is that time period matched to your own? If not, how does it differ?

   _____

   _____

   _____

3. If not, what might you do to affect the alignment or to compensate for the nonalignment?

   _____

   _____

   _____

   _____

   _____

   _____

   _____

   _____

Do It Now!

The clock below shows divisions in the workday rather than the usual hourly sequence. Circle in red the hour in each quadrant when you're operating at peak-performance levels. Circle in blue the hour in each quadrant when you find yourself at your lowest energy level. Then write in the kinds of tasks appropriate to each.

Red activity _____   **Red activity** _____

Blue _____   **Blue** _____

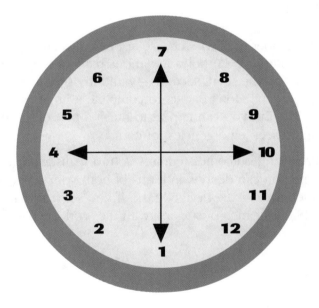

Red activity _____   **Red activity** _____

Blue _____   **Blue** _____

Week 28:
Commit to finishing at least a segment of a project or task.

Theophrasteus: "Time is the most valuable thing a man can spend."

Remember the Swiss cheese approach to taming projects of the first magnitude? Poke holes in various parts of the project's body and work on the small sections—without worrying about the project in its entirety. Don't expect to complete a huge assignment in one sitting. But you can expect to finish a part of the project, barring unforeseen emergencies, of course.

Projecting outcomes requires you to realistically assess how much time you can devote, in terms of both your schedule and your tolerance for the disliked task. If you set reasonable goals, you have a better chance of sticking with the work segment until you meet your objective.

Action Questions

1. Have you established lifetime goals? _____

2. If so, have you written them down? _____

   (One research study found that people with recorded goals were earning ten times more than people with no goals at all.)

3. Write some of the goals for your life that are most important to you: _____

   _____

   _____

   _____

   _____

   _____

   _____

   _____

   _____

   _____

   _____

   _____

   _____

4. Do you typically break down your goals into the tasks or activities you need to do to achieve those goals? _____

5. If not, choose one of your life goals and outline a step-by-step plan for accomplishing it. Do the "mini" goals you listed in each step seem more manageable than the large, overall goal?

_____

_____

_____

_____

_____

_____

_____

_____

_____

_____

Do It Now!

Answer True or False to the following.

1. I believe that most work requires completion rather than perfection. T F

2. I am fairly accurate in predicting what I can accomplish in a particular time frame. T F

3. I don't like leaving things unfinished. T F

4. I don't let interruptions take me away from my intended accomplishments. T F

5. I pride myself on my perseverance. T F

If the majority of your answers are "true," it would appear you have a good grasp of the Swiss cheese approach. Have you considered becoming an "efficiency exemplar?" In what ways—publicly or not—could you share with others what you have learned about segmenting a large project?

_____

_____

_____

_____

If the majority of your answers are "false," think about what you could do or whom you could consult to convert the "falses" to "trues." Record your thoughts here:

_____

_____

_____

_____

Week 29:
Realistically appraise how much time a dreaded task will require.

Peter Drucker: "Time—unless it is managed, nothing else can be managed."

Animals have barks that are worse than their bites. So do tasks, in a manner of speaking. They often are less odious than you may at first anticipate. Some people dislike preparing taxes so much, for example, that they file for extension after extension. In truth, the average tax return can be completed in less than one weekend.

Sit down and map out how long it will take you to complete a dreaded job. If it's a job you're facing for the first time, speak with others who've done a similar job so you can realistically assess the task. Once you have an idea of how much time you'll need, you can begin to assign milestone dates for completing various parts of the job.

Action Questions

1. Think about your typical work style. Do you estimate how long it will take you to do a job before you start it? If so, how often are you correct? If you don't, what's preventing you from doing so?

_____

_____

_____

_____

_____

_____

2. Can you recall some instances when the actual time to do the task you'd been procrastinating required much less than what you'd imagined?

_____

_____

_____

_____

Do It Now!

To develop your ability to accurately estimate time requirements, at least once a day, make a prediction about the length of time a particular activity will take before you complete it. For example, if you are driving to work, note the time you leave your driveway. Then mentally calculate: "I should be at the corner of Main and Exchange ten minutes from now." When you get there, see how close you were to the mark. Or, once you are at work and have begun to compose a letter, estimate: "I should have this done by 9:15." When you have finished, note the time. Continue with your temporal gauges until you find you are very, very good at making these kinds of projections.

Week 30:

Log the time you waste—time you could use to finish a task you've been procrastinating.

Mad Hatter: "If you knew Time as well as I do, you wouldn't talk about wasting it."

As well as you think you know yourself, you may be surprised to learn that you're spending your days in ways other than what you intended. You may be shaking your head right now and thinking, "That may be true for others, but it would never be true of me." It may be more true than you think.

Once you know where you're wasting time, you'll have a larger inventory of minutes to spend on the tasks that you haven't been able to get done because you "just can't find the time to do them."

Action Questions

1. Before you begin the log described in the Do It Now! exercise, make a prediction: What do you think your biggest time-wasters are?

_____

_____

_____

_____

_____

_____

2. In terms of your answer to #1, how can you "be ruthless with time but gracious with people"? (This is standard advice for time managers.)

_____

_____

_____

_____

_____

Do It Now!

According to a nationwide survey by Accountemps, the average worker is wasting as much as a third of every workday. (This would mean employees are paid for a full seventeen weeks of work during which they don't produce anything.) So you *are* wasting *some* time. We all do.

For *at least* one full day, jot down the number of minutes you spend on things that don't need to be done at all or that could be done more efficiently. Include meetings from which you derive little benefit or writing reports that no one reads. You get the picture.

When you have at least twenty items on the list, go back and see which of the items you can do something about.

Comments from Gwen Brock, Executive Secretary, Northrop-Grumman Corporation

I am a firm believer in not taxing my brain (whenever I can avoid doing so). To accomplish this, I use a daily planner in the office. I plan my day the evening before, when the office is quiet and my boss has left for the day. Always beginning with the most critical project first, then an easy but necessary project, I experience accomplishment right away and get two projects behind me immediately.

Because the time of secretaries and administrative assistants is never their own—they are constantly interrupted by phones and people—it's important to:

1. Prepare the night before for the next day.

2. Prioritize your work.

3. Be purposeful about what will get done when.

Procrastination always gets you in trouble. It never fails. The one time that you "put it off until tomorrow" is the time you needed to get it done the day before. As soon as I receive an assignment, I set up a file folder with that project's name. In it, I put my transcribed instructions or my own notes and a timetable for estimated completion.

Trying to accomplish as much as possible while the project assignment is fresh in your mind is always better than procrastinating what needs to be done. This is especially true when handling domestic or international travel. Into the file should go what the boss wants, what the hotel advises, what the travel agent says, what the airline detailed, and so on. All these things make the ultimate completion of the task much easier.

The advice also applies to an assignment given to your boss by his or her boss. Prepare the file, gather as much information as you can for your boss on the subject, and give him or her periodic updates and reminders.

Week 31:
Develop a routine.

Charles M. Schwab: "I had put off a phone call for nine months, so I decided to list it as my number one task on my next day's agenda. That call netted us a $2 million order."

The simplest techniques are often the most powerful in terms of the results achieved. Charles Schwab, then chairman of Bethlehem Steel, followed the advice of a management consultant to prepare a daily "To Do" list and complete the priorities on it. He asked the consultant what he owed him and the consultant replied, "Try it for six months and then pay me what you think it is worth." Six months later, the consultant received a check for $25,000. Not bad for a four-word recommendation ("Things To Do Today").

Use the familiar To Do list or establish a routine of your own. One good technique, for example, is to make a one-page copy of a calendar showing the next twelve months. Set a goal, such as exercising four times a week, and then place a happy face on the dates you do but an angry red mark on the dates you don't. You'll find your internal wish to write in four happy faces a week strong enough to propel you toward movement—especially if you keep your calendar visible at all times.

Having a routine and sticking to it provides great leverage for moving metaphorical mountains.

Action Questions

1. In what areas of your life do you follow a fairly strict routine?

   _____

   _____

   _____

   _____

   _____

   _____

2. What "crutches" (such as posting a calendar with angry red marks) might help you establish a routine for tasks you procrastinate?

   _____

   _____

   _____

   _____

   _____

   _____

Do It Now!

Memorize this anonymous quotation and make it the beginning of your daily routine:

This day is for you—rejoice in it.

This day is for tomorrow—treasure its memory.

Week 32:
Remind yourself that you have as much time as anyone else (but you may be wasting more!).

Anonymous: "People who make the worst use of their time are the same ones who complain that there is never enough time."

It's easy to complain about how much you have to do and how little time you have to do it in. You may find that you grumble less, however, if you occasionally remind yourself that even the President of the United States, with a country to run and a world of worries, finds time to play golf every now and then.

We're all given the same gift of time—24 hours a day—and yet some people use it to great advantage while others complain about the inadequacy of the gift. Admit that you're probably doing some things wrong, but also some things right. Continue doing the things you're doing right. Eliminate or change what you're doing wrong. And periodically remind yourself that you have as much time as anyone else. The real question is not how *much* you have but what you do with what you have.

Action Questions

1. Beginning this very moment and continuing for the next seven days, ask yourself this question several times a day: "Am I making the very best use of my time at this moment?"

   Over the seven-day period, how many times did you answer "Yes"? _____

   How many times did you answer "No"? _____

   Do this for several weeks until a majority of "yes" answers begins to emerge.

2. The very best use of your time at a given moment may in fact find you doing nothing at all. How many times during the week were you using your time to relieve stress or recharge your batteries so you could continue to work in a more productive fashion? _____

Do It Now!

Use the "Four-T" technique whenever the procrastination monster is breathing down your neck. Ask yourself, is the work:

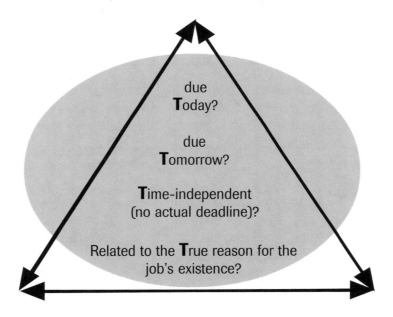

due **T**oday?

due **T**omorrow?

Time-independent
(no actual deadline)?

Related to the **T**rue reason for the
job's existence?

Sometimes, when your adrenaline is pumping and you're "pumped up" for battle with the Procrastination Monster, you may unnecessarily burden yourself with work that truly is postponable, even work that perhaps is unnecessary. The Four Ts will help bring perspective to your decisions regarding which work to attack and when.

Week 33:
Learn to manage your own time and stop blaming others.

Charles Dickens: "Father Time is not always a hard parent, and, though he tarries for none of his children, often lays his hand lightly on those who have used him well."

To some extent it's true that others influence how we spend our time. The mother who wants to read a magazine while her child is screaming for breakfast knows that motherhood dictates her time. Or the manager who fully intends to work on an overdue budget but whose boss is calling for a different report also knows that being an employee means sometimes conforming to the wishes of others.

No matter what you do in life, though, some of your time is discretionary. Look at what you can control and refuse to blame others for what you cannot.

Sometimes the secret to wise time management or effective breaking of the procrastination habit is to shave time off one activity and apply it to another. We all have to sleep, of course. But is it possible for you to relinquish twenty minutes a day—or every other day—and use that time for a project you keep meaning to do? More than likely, the answer is yes.

We all need to eat, of course, but is it possible for you to skip one meal a week and use that time for a long-postponed task? Again this is possible for most of us.

If you call a favorite friend or faraway relative every Sunday and chat for a long time, could you skip just one Sunday and use the time for a task you fear will never get done?

Whatever your schedule is like, it will probably allow contracting and expanding so you can remove items from your procrastination list, one at a time.

Action Questions

1. Assume you've won the lottery and don't have to work. What will you do with your time?

   _____

   _____

   _____

   _____

   _____

   _____

2. How could you alter your current patterns so that the activities you mentioned in #1 could play a greater role than they do in your life right now?

   _____

   _____

   _____

   _____

   _____

   _____

Do It Now!

In the left-hand column, circle the letter "A" if you agree with the statement and "D" if you disagree.

How I View Myself

**Agree/
Disagree**

A   D   1. I tend to view myself as a victim.

A   D   2. I complain more than the average person does.

A   D   3. I regard myself as a resourceful person.

A   D   4. I would say I am a punctual person.

A   D   5. I tend to use excuses to explain why things didn't get done rather than take action to get them done.

Now, make seven copies of the following list. Write your name in the blank space and distribute the copies to seven people you know well. They should be individuals who care enough about you to be honest and yet can express their honesty in a caring way. If you can, select easygoing people with a good sense of humor. They will need to be the metaphoric Novocain in the dentist-like exercise you will be putting yourself through.

Ask them to circle "A" if they agree with the statement about you and "D" if they disagree.

How Others View Me

**Agree/
Disagree**

A   D   1.   _____ tends to view him-/herself as a victim.

A   D   2.   _____ complains more than the average person does.

A   D   3.   _____ is resourceful.

A   D   4.   _____ is punctual.

A   D   5.   _____ tends to use excuses rather than action.

The final stage can be handled in two ways. You can ask your friends to mail you their responses and then you can read them privately. Or you can assemble the friends and hold a discussion about improving their perceptions, especially if their collective opinion differs markedly from your own.

Week 34:
Ask yourself "reality check" questions before you decide to postpone a task.

Peter Drucker: "Everything requires time. It is the only truly universal condition. All work takes place in time and uses up time. Yet most people take for granted this unique, irreplaceable, and necessary resource. Nothing else, perhaps, distinguishes effective executives as much as their tender loving care of time."

Doing a reality check often is enough to sway you from a potentially disastrous course of action. The reality check for you in Week 34 consists of the Action Questions. Answering them will often keep the Procrastination Monster at bay. It might be fun and fruitful to ask a colleague, perhaps even your manager, to add some questions to the list.

Try this technique for a week. Use it on the next task that beckons you to procrastinate.

Action Questions

1. Do I really want to postpone this? _____

2. Do I really need to postpone this? _____

3. What would my boss say if he or she knew I was contemplating procrastination? _____
   _____

4. If this job were facing my CEO, would he or she be postponing it?
   _____

5. What will happen if I postpone the job?
   _____

6. If I postpone it now, when will I find time to do it later?
   _____

7. Could I do just a small part of it now? _____
   Which part? _____

8. Is there someone I could call who would tell me to get going on it? Who?
   _____

9. How many times have I already procrastinated with this assignment?
   _____

10. If I do procrastinate now, what better use will I make of the time I've gained?
    _____

Do It Now!

At what time of day are you most likely to procrastinate? _____

At what time are you least likely to procrastinate? _____

Read the following research about "chronobiology" and see if your responses to the previous questions are in line with the research findings. Try altering your usual procedures in light of what the research reveals about the effect of time upon physical actions.

- Best decision-making time: Before noon

- Worst decision-making time: Between 2 p.m. and 8 p.m.

- Time of least depression: Between 7 a.m. and 11 a.m.

- Time of most anxiety: Between 2 p.m. and 8 p.m.

- Best time for working on complex tasks: Between noon and late afternoon

- Best time for short-term memory: Between 10 a.m. and 11 a.m.

- Best time for long-term memory: Between noon and 3 p.m.

- Best time to acquire knowledge: Before going to sleep

- Best time to ask for a raise: During lunch

Based on this information, record here one change you might try incorporating into your daily schedule to increase productivity:

_____

_____

_____

_____

Week 35:
Advance the action on several projects at once.

Etty Allen commenting on her husband George's hatred of time-wasteful actions: "His favorite food is ice cream because he doesn't have to chew it."

One technique employed by those who most soundly defeat procrastination is the "Advancing Multiple Actions (AMA)" approach. It works like this: Assume you are honor-bound to work one hour today on a task that you've been putting off and putting off. You could even add three other such tasks. Then, rather than working for a full hour on the dreaded, dreary job, you can spread your energy by splitting the hour into four parts and working on all four projects during that time, each for fifteen minutes.

After four days, you will have the same results (perhaps even better results) than if you had tackled each of the projects for one hour each on four sequential days.

Action Questions

1. Are you a person who is easily bored? If so, what are your anti-boredom strategies?

_____

_____

_____

_____

2. If you aren't, how do you maximize your ability to do the same thing for a prolonged period?

_____

_____

_____

_____

3. What do you think is the connection between channel-surfing and the AMA Approach?

_____

_____

_____

_____

Do It Now!

In the "Project Pie" shown below, write the names of six major tasks you need to accomplish in the next ten working days.

Project Pie

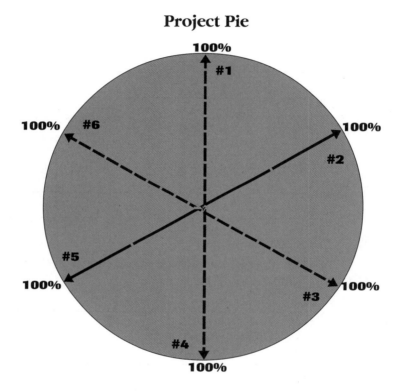

You will note there are ten notches in the line beside each number (representing increments of 10 percent, which when accumulated, will mean the project is 100 percent complete). At the end of every day, show (with different-colored markers) how far you have advanced the project. If the projects are ongoing, covering a multiple-week or multiple-month span, make enough copies of the "Project Pie" to last the duration of the longest-running assignment.

Week 36:
Tell people you can't be interrupted unless it's an emergency.

Samuel Goldwyn: "For as long as I can remember, whatever I was doing at the time was the most important thing in the world for me."

Obviously, the better your interpersonal relationships, the more easily you will be able to use this tool. Once you've begun to use it, though, others will learn how serious you are and it will be easier to establish a routine for its use. You must set limits on your noninterruptible time, of course, and you must be reachable should you truly be needed. But you will surprise yourself (perhaps others as well) with how much you can get done when you close yourself off once a day or even once a week. Schedule your less-than-enjoyable tasks for this time. Put on your metaphoric ear plugs so you can't hear the sirens' song—and then get to work.

Action Questions

1. Jot down a script you might use to explain to people why you don't want to be interrupted. Knowing in advance what you will say makes it easier to be "gracious with people but ruthless with time."

_____

_____

_____

_____

_____

2. When was the last real emergency that occurred in your work environment? For what kinds of "urgencies" would you want to be interrupted?

_____

_____

_____

_____

_____

_____

_____

Do It Now!

This exercise requires a long piece of rope or yarn. When you next face a job that must get done and you can't procrastinate a minute longer, get settled and make certain you have everything with you that you'll need to do the job (or a segment of it). Put a sign on your door ("Not now, please") and turn on your answering machine or voice mail. Take the yarn and tie one end around your wrist and the other end to a solid stationary object in your office. Get to work. Soon you'll be tempted to go make copies, make a call, or get an extra file. The yarn will help you resist the urge.

The actual effort required to untie the rope will usually be enough to deter you. Of course, you'll need a break at some point. But generally speaking, the rope and you should remain tethered to each other until you've finished the chunk of work you've committed yourself to.

Week 37:
Train others so you can share the tasks you dislike.

Margaret McElroy: "Poor delegation is a major cause for lost time."

Organizations are filled with people who are too busy to learn how to become less busy. They manage time poorly, yet feel they don't have time for time management classes. *You* are clearly an exception, as you are taking the time to overcome these inclinations by reading this book and changing your habits.

However, there's more to be done. It's true that taking the time to train others will slow you down in the short run; however, it will speed you up in the long run. If, for example, you're the person everyone runs to when the copy machine breaks or the computer acts up, you're providing a valued service to others—but at a cost to your own efficiency. If *many* people know how to fix the breakdowns, though, the dependence on you as the equipment wizard will lessen.

Individual obligation is diminished when a bothersome or disliked task is shared.

Action Questions

1. Is vanity causing you to do some things that others really should be doing? Explain.

_____

_____

_____

_____

_____

_____

_____

2. What excuses do employees use to take the "responsibility monkey" off their own backs and put it on someone else's?

_____

_____

_____

_____

_____

_____

_____

_____

_____

Do It Now!

Answer the following questions "true" or "false."

	True	False
1. I like the feeling of being needed by other people.	_____	_____
2. I honestly don't mind helping others out.	_____	_____
3. It's usually quicker to do something myself than to show others how.	_____	_____
4. I don't regard myself as a teacher or trainer.	_____	_____
5. I suspect I'm working harder, not smarter.	_____	_____

Having three or more "true" answers indicates some improvement is needed. Admittedly, it is a good feeling to know that others depend on us. But when patterns of overdependency begin emerging, we have to recall the word "purpose." The purpose behind your hiring was not altruism or assisting others whenever they come running. The purpose was for you to get your work done as efficiently as possible. And if you are taking on too much work, if you have an "I-can-do-it-all" attitude, you may be negatively impacting your own productivity. You may also be impacting the potential productivity of co-workers.

Week 38:
Make difficult assignments team assignments when you can.

Nikolai Lenin: "One hundred organized men can always defeat one thousand disorganized ones."

Many hands, says the proverb, make light work. Not all projects, but certainly some, could be better completed with group effort. How do you decide which ones? Use these guidelines:

- Work you find especially tiresome
- Work requiring talents or knowledge that others possess to a greater degree than you do
- Work with components that can be broken down or easily divided
- Work needed to respond to a crisis
- Work that would help develop team cohesion
- Work that you couldn't do (or do well) alone by the given deadline

Action Questions

1. What additional guidelines could you use to determine team assignments?

   _____

   _____

   _____

   _____

2. Select three guidelines from the preceding page, convert them to questions, and answer them here. For example, the first guideline, if you chose it, would become "What work do I find especially tiresome?"

   1st Question: _____

   _____

   Response: _____

   _____

   2nd Question: _____

   _____

   Response: _____

   _____

   3rd Question: _____

   _____

   Response: _____

   _____

Do It Now!

To decide how to distribute the work associated with a particularly burdensome task, follow these steps:

1. Analyze the task in terms of the skills required to complete its various components. For example, some aspects of the task might require analytical skills; others might require persuasive skills.

2. Convene eight to ten people who have agreed in advance to be part of an ongoing shared-work team. Ask each person to write down the type of task he or she most enjoys doing.

3. Align the talent with the components of the project.

Week 39:
Turn off the phone for a while.

Elizabeth Akers Allen: "Backward, turn backward, O Time, in your flight. Make me a child again, just for tonight!"

Remember how deeply you were able to concentrate on games that you played as a child? Remember the intensity with which you imagined scenarios to fill your play time, characters to be your friends, adventures to be lived as you read about them? During those times, you were able to keep the outside world from intruding on your activity. You still *have* the ability to delve deeply into the setting before you.

To help you escape the external world so you can explore the inner one, try shutting off the phones for a while. Have someone else cover them. Or use voice mail or electronic mail to let the messages pile up while you think deeply and creatively.

Action Questions

1. If your boss had asked you to make a brief presentation to new hires on ways to use voice mail most efficiently, what points would you make? Once you have your key points in place, apply them to your own situation.

_____

_____

_____

_____

_____

_____

_____

_____

2. Under what circumstances could leaving a voice mail message be preferable to direct conversation?

_____

_____

_____

_____

Do It Now!

Here's a general rule for avoiding procrastination and focusing on the "vital few" aspects of your job instead of the "trivial many":

"Don't major in the minors!"

A "Do and Don't" list, especially if written succinctly, serves as an excellent reminder of your purpose for undertaking any task. You can create such a list to help you focus on virtually any work enterprise, but for your mission here, begin thinking about do's and don'ts that could help you use telephone turn-off time to escape the Procrastination Monster and to major in the majors.

The next page provides a few for openers. Continue to add to the list as you learn how best to use this procrastination-defeating tool. When the list is as complete as it can be, share it with others, perhaps via your organization's newsletter. (*Caution:* Don't simply make the "Don't" column the opposite of the "Do" points. Think more deeply than that.)

Telephone Do's & Don'ts

Do	Don't
Have an alternative, such as an answering machine for messages.	Forget to check for messages periodically.
Arrange a way others can reach you in case of a true emergency.	Waste this ideal time.
Try to establish the phone-free time at the same time every day.	Make yourself unreachable for too long.

_____   _____

_____   _____

_____   _____

_____   _____

_____   _____

_____   _____

_____   _____

_____   _____

_____   _____

_____   _____

Week 40:
Develop Pavlovian practices.

Virgil: "Time bears away all things, even our minds."

Time is more valuable than money. Should you doubt the truth of this, think about a millionaire facing death: all the money in the world can't buy him or her more time. And yet, you have time that he or she doesn't. Spend it well. One way to ward off procrastination is to develop Pavlovian practices; that is, condition yourself to respond with a certain activity when faced with certain types of situations.

For example, one Pavlovian practice you'll probably find beneficial requires you to always have paper and pen nearby. Then when you can see a wait coming on, reach for the paper and begin writing. Outline your shopping list, your goals, the introductory paragraph for your next report, even an anecdote you can send in to *Reader's Digest* and possibly earn some money for. Be like Noel Coward, who when caught in a traffic jam, pulled out a sheet of paper and wrote the popular tune, "I'll See You Again."

The "Just write!" technique isn't the only one you should train yourself to follow. There are numerous others. Find some others that prompt you to do something positive to ward off what would be wasted time.

Action Questions

Consider Pavlovian practices you could develop for the following situations:

- Someone dominates the meeting by elaborating excessively on a point:

  _____

  _____

  _____

  _____

- Work becomes monotonous:

  _____

  _____

  _____

  _____

- Your energy levels start to slip:

  _____

  _____

  _____

  _____

Do It Now!

Find a recording of music you find highly energizing. Try keeping a tape recorder and this recording at work for the next week. Each day, quietly play the song several times and get in the habit of responding to it. During that time, condition yourself to work as hard and as fast as you can on the most difficult aspect of a project facing you.

Comments from Susan Anselm, Account Executive, DATAMAX Services, Inc.

In my youth, I typically put off papers for school until the last minute. Then in my twenties, I found that I could do almost twice as much as I had ever tried before by keeping a fast pace and being constantly active. My values and sensitivities affected my prioritization. This helped me contribute effectively to community organizing, but caused me difficulty in dealing with other uninteresting work, like paying bills on time or housekeeping chores. I have always been motivated by exciting or challenging work.

At the end of my twenties, I became a single parent. Then, time management became absolutely critical. I learned to let go of truly unimportant things and to make other things important. Structure and scheduling were key. I parented, worked full time, and continued my education all at the same time. The most significant rule that I learned was to do first those things I dreaded or disliked most. Then they impacted only a small part of my day. If you put off the things you least like, you think about them all day and they don't improve the quality of the day.

After twenty years of counseling experience, I finally learned to take my own advice. If a task overwhelms me, I break it down into parts and complete it piece by piece. This way, I have the satisfaction of making progress; completing one small piece motivates me to move on to another. Many people delay or stonewall when they feel overwhelmed. But, you can control your environment to some extent and so control your reluctance. You *can* self-motivate.

With total quiet, no interruptions, and the practice of visualization, I can study and remember important material with relative ease. I no longer need last-minute "cramming" for tests. Lists are helpful to ensure nothing gets overlooked, and they're great for feeling successful when you cross items off. However, sometimes we rob ourselves of these good feelings by noticing only what still needs to be done.

Significant to my time management efforts is my practice of a twelve-step program. Taking things "one day at a time" makes the work of each day more manageable. No one can arbitrarily extend a day beyond twenty-four hours. Accepting both what I can manage and what I can't relieves me from wasting mental energy trying to control things over which I have no control. I recommend that people separate their responsibilities from those of others. Doing this opens up a lot of time for those who tend to "take care of others." Make sure your "have-to" obligations really have to be done by you.

I recently changed jobs. I had been working for a not-for-profit agency and truly liked my work. The group I worked with could move with speed and direction. From idea inception to completion, we planned a new curriculum; brought competitive vendors and suppliers together to collaborate on donating $600,000 of hardware, software, and peripherals; and built a learning lab of connectivity and interoperability. It was an environment desirable to business but one with no precedent. From start to finish, this effort took five-and-a-half months.

In contrast, I have worked in bureaucracies that took three months to approve a one-page document and places that provided vague expectations of the end product. In such places, it seems that everyone who touches a document is compelled to change it. There is no trust of anyone else's authorship. Consequently, without collaboration, administration might make commitments to other sectors of the business community and then miss their targets by months, with no concern about the effect on credibility. Practices of this kind can hurt reputations. People who flourish in such an atmosphere believe, I suspect, that the longer it takes a person to get something off his or her desk, the more the task can be viewed as one requiring lengthy deliberation. Few people are fooled though.

I chose DATAMAX as my current employer because of its integrity and also because the company can and does move quickly in response to customers' needs. Emerging technologies are examined quickly. The company is flexible and can change directions in a minute if necessary or can find the additional resources necessary to change strategic direction. DATAMAX uncovers potential opportunities and creatively plan ways to take advantage of them.

I believe one of the major reasons for its success is that DATAMAX takes calculated risks but does not spend excessive time to be 100 percent certain something will work before it is tried. Couple this with the ability to change or try another method, and delays are minimal.

Some people are so cautious that they defer decisions to be on the safe side. Consequently, they miss too many opportunities. They have never-ending lists. Such behavior is self-defeating. Today's business environment is changing almost as fast as technology. Slow and steady does not win the race. It only makes the competitor as obsolete as yesterday's computer.

Twelve-steppers say "Progress, not perfection." I've met many people who will put something off until it "can be done perfectly." If perfection were possible, continuous improvement would be unnecessary. "Do it right the first time" does not mean "do it perfectly." "Do it right and be willing to improve it" is realistic.

The folks I've known who have the worst procrastination problems spend endless hours thinking about what they need to do. Not *some* time for planning, but long times, so that they're tired of the problem before they even begin to solve it. Once the resistance to getting started is overcome, they can become efficient. But, overplanning for a changing environment just isn't a good use of time.

Know how you work best, and at what, and then sculpt your job for the best possible fit. In other words, play on your strengths and minimize your weaknesses. The team environment lends itself to this quite well. Not everyone needs to be equally good at everything. Stack the deck with team decisions on who does what and why, rather than adhere to job descriptions or hierarchical structures. I know I'm excellent at initiating action or innovation and I struggle with meticulous, detail-driven work. I know what I can contribute to a team.

Finally, remember that in adult life, there's no such thing as being totally caught up!

Week 41:
Learn how to make yourself feel guilty.

Shakespeare: "O! call back yesterday, bid time return."

Not everyone is adept at inflicting self-guilt. However, with enough practice, you should very soon know how to push your own guilt buttons. It may help to recall the story of H.L. Hunt, who gave up smoking his beloved cigars, but not for the reason you may think. He had calculated that the time it took to unwrap the cigars—time he could have spent working—was costing him about a third of a million dollars a year.

Who knows how much you are losing? It might be eye-opening to do some calculations of your own. If guilt results, use it—as Hunt did—to break some bad habits.

Action Questions

1. Think about people who make you feel guilty. What exactly do they make you feel guilty *about?*

   _____

   _____

   _____

   _____

   _____

   _____

   _____

2. How could you capitalize on those feelings in terms of gaining control of your procrastinating inclinations?

   _____

   _____

   _____

   _____

Do It Now!

Compose ten guilt-ridden statements and write one each on ten adhesive notes. Have a close friend or family member do the same. (The more you have, the better this Do It Now! exercise will work.) Sample guilt-goaders might be:

Remember all the trouble you created for yourself the last time you procrastinated?

He who procrastinates is lost. Find yourself—immediately!

Procrastination today, purgatory tomorrow.

Procrastination is a curable disease.

Don't put it off—put it on *your desk* now!

Post these statements in unusual places (or have a friend do this for you from time to time) so that you will be surprised by the anti-procrastination reminders. And, yes, so that you'll feel guilty enough to get going.

Week 42:
Build in spare moments or contingency time.

Edward FitzGerald: "The Bird of Time has but a little way to fly."

Experts agree: Days that are too full can make you counterproductive. You end up feeling "wired" or overcommitted. Rather than using time masterfully, you wind up frittering it away by rushing from one commitment to the next (and making mistakes along the way).

Allow time each day for doing no more than thinking—thinking about what must be done with your day, thinking about goals, thinking about how you will use the spare half-hour or hour that you have built in for reflection. At the end of the day, if you've had no reason to use the tucked-away time, you can always put it to good use by getting some of tomorrow's chores done or by doing some of the tasks that you always seem to put off (filing, reading, etc.) because they have no real immediacy.

Action Questions

1. How much quiet time do you allow yourself (both personally and professionally) each week (time that is not scheduled for anything or anyone but you)?

   _____

   _____

2. You know about Murphy's law. It applies to procrastinators too. If you wait until the last minute, the copy machine will be broken, the computer will be down, or the secretary will be out sick. What laws like Murphy's have you come upon in your own work experience?

   _____

   _____

   _____

   _____

   _____

   _____

   _____

   _____

   _____

Do It Now!

1. Who is the most efficient person you know?

   _____

2. If you could place a tap on his or her phone for a week, what would you hear?

   _____

   _____

   _____

   _____

3. If he or she placed a tap on *your* phone for a week, what would be heard?

   _____

   _____

   _____

   _____

4. What did you learn from this introspection?

   _____

   _____

   _____

   _____

Week 43:
Get a shadow.

Seneca: "Time discovers truth."

Especially a shadow whose judgment you trust. The shadow will see or hear you as you can't see or hear yourself because you're too involved in your work to be aware of what you're doing. The shadow is like the fly on the wall who can tell you more than you may want to know, but things you need to hear.

Action Questions

1. The most valuable insights the shadow can provide will be based on your typical actions, not those that are made to look good for his or her benefit. To what degree could you go through a day as you usually do, even though someone is watching your every move?

_____

_____

_____

_____

2. How defensive a person are you?

_____

_____

_____

Do It Now!

According to *Fortune* magazine (vol. 126, no. 16, "The Executive's New Coach"), executives pay as much as $1,500 for a single-day program ($100,000 or more for a multi-year coaching program) designed to help managers with personality problems succeed. If you are a person interested in continuous improvement, especially as far as productivity is concerned, you may want to persuade a friend (inside or outside the company) to shadow you for a day (or part of a day).

Your shadow will simply observe you as you interact, doing the things you always do in the way you always do them. The shadow does not offer any feedback until the post-shadowing conference. Essentially, your shadow makes notes in these three areas:

1. Strengths (to be continued)

_____

_____

_____

_____

_____

2. Weaknesses (to be eliminated)

_____

_____

_____

_____

_____

_____

3. Ideas (to be explored)

_____

_____

_____

_____

_____

_____

Week 44:
Let go of perfectionism.

Franklin Delano Roosevelt: "Perfectionism . . . may obstruct the paths to international peace."

While the desire to be spectacularly good at everything you do is a noble one, it can also be a destructive one. Those who wish to have it all and be it all usually wind up frustrating themselves and aggravating others. There is a time when "good enough" really is "good enough." Remembering to strive for excellence rather than perfectionism enables you to do more in less time. It also helps you tackle jobs that seem more daunting than they really are.

Action Questions

1. What kind of work do you think requires absolute perfection on your part?

_____

_____

_____

_____

_____

2. What kinds of stresses/fears does the perfectionist face?

_____

_____

_____

_____

_____

3. What would happen if you decided to strive for "excellence" in the work you listed in #1 above rather than perfectionism?

_____

_____

_____

_____

_____

Do It Now!

Answer the questions that follow. Then put the paper aside for two months. Return to it after you have finished all the skill-building exercises in this book. You may be mildly surprised when you see what you wrote here for Week 44. You should do one more thing now. Ask a family member to guess what you wrote to complete these five statements. Then share your actual responses with that person, discussing the discrepancies between your answers.

1. The *real* cause of my procrastination habit is:

   _____

   _____

2. My boss would describe my procrastination tendencies as:

   _____

   _____

3. People who procrastinate are usually:

   _____

   _____

4. I am inclined/am not inclined (circle one) to be a perfectionist because:

   _____

   _____

5. If I cut procrastination by 10 percent this week:

   _____

   _____

Week 45:
Find an even more odious task that has to be done so the current one pales by comparison.

Winston Churchill: " ... we learn that ... something is going on in space and time, and beyond space and time, which, whether we like it or not, spells duty."

Surely, there's something in your life that needs doing, something you've been putting off for any number of reasons. You can continue putting it off *if* you are willing to do something that's even more distasteful. For example, if there's a closet that really needs to be cleaned out and you're resisting the chore, resist some more. But you must pledge to clean out the attic instead.

Given the choice between the work you've been putting off and a really off-putting task (doesn't that oven need to be cleaned in the employee kitchen?), most people will opt to do the work that is less unpleasant.

Action Questions

1. What are some of the most unpleasant tasks you can think of?

_____

_____

_____

_____

_____

2. Which ones are even more unpleasant?

_____

_____

_____

_____

_____

Do It Now!

Should you join the Procrastinators Club?

Answer the following questions "true" or "false."

	True	False
1. Twenty-five percent of adults are serious procrastinators.	_____	_____
2. The Procrastinators Club has 9,000 members.	_____	_____
3. Its president estimates an additional 500,000 have been putting off enrolling in the club.	_____	_____
4. The Club celebrates the Fourth of July in January.	_____	_____
5. You can join by writing them at Box 712, Bryn Athyn, PA 19009.	_____	_____

Just as tall people join the tall people's club for a sense of association with kindred spirits and kindred sizes, procrastinators can associate and celebrate with others like themselves too. (Yes, the address is accurate and yes, all the answers above are true.) Be forewarned, however, the procrastinators are more interested in fun than in reforming their ways.

Week 46:
Variety is the ice of strife.

Thomas Mann: "Time cools, time clarifies; no mood can be maintained quite unaltered through the course of hours."

We live in an era where the tempo of daily living is quick and the pressures prevalent. The heat generated by stress, though, can be cooled with variety. For example, if you have an eight-hour day ahead of you with fourteen things you must get done, make it an eight-hour-and-ten-minute day and increase the number of things to sixteen. The new inclusions will be things you love to do but always say you don't have time for.

Are you a frustrated artist? Well, between terrible task #4 and terrible task #5, insert a five-minute drawing lesson. You claim you never have time to read biographies of artists? When you finish terrible task #11 and before you begin #12, pick up a book and read for five minutes.

Not only should you spread the variety around in this way, you should also spread it among the sequence of tasks. Don't do seven tasks in a row that call for mind-numbing work, such as working with figures. Do a few of those and then change to tasks that call for physical actions or social interactions.

Action Questions

1. How many different types of work do you do? List them here.

_____

_____

_____

_____

_____

_____

2. What is your typical working style?

_____

_____

_____

_____

_____

_____

Do It Now!

Your daily sequence of tasks should always include something physical, preferably something that is good for your health and an interesting diversion at the same time. When you need a break between terrible tasks # 3 and #4, try standing and swinging your arms briskly—as if you were walking along at a rapid clip. The motion is good for circulation and for clearing the head of the cobwebs of which headaches are spun. Do this for several minutes before returning to your desk.

Week 47:

Determine an objective to be accomplished each morning and each afternoon.

Kathryn McNeill: "Make your desk a one-stop shopping area."

If, like William Handy, you "hate to see the evenin' sun go down," it may be because you feel the day did not yield the results it should have. To provide clarity to your purpose and give your action direction, articulate one thing you definitely wish to get done each morning and one thing you want to have completed by the end of the afternoon.

To increase the likelihood of this happening, you will want to have near you everything you need for completing the various steps in the process. When you find yourself jumping up to locate various supplies or files, you may also find that you don't return to the project at hand.

Action Questions

1. How much thinking do you do each day about *what* you will do each day?

   _____

2. If your answer is "at least fifteen minutes," then you probably have learned to balance priorities and achieve them as well. Yet, because we live in an era of continuous improvement, we know we can always sharpen our abilities. How might you optimize the time you currently spend planning each day?

   _____

   _____

   _____

   _____

   _____

   _____

3. If your answer is "I don't spend any time thinking about what to do. I just do what needs to be done," then it's time for you to form a new habit. Psychologists tell us that we need two weeks for a habit to become ingrained. On your calendar, block off a ten- or fifteen-minute period at the beginning or end of each day. (Make certain to put the calendar where you can see it easily.) Plan to review priorities during this time each and every day for the next two weeks. Keep these questions in mind as you do so:

   - If nothing else gets done today, what *must* get done?

   - What have I learned about living, based on what I did yesterday?

Do It Now!

A centarian was once asked his secret of longevity. His response was logical and short-winded. "Just keep breathing!" As you work to overcome the normal inclination to put off work, you will find that some techniques work better for you than others do. By this point in the year, you should have discovered some tools that help you set and reach objectives, whether they are daily or weekly or project-related ones. Consider the following question:

"What is your secret for keeping the Procrastination Monster at bay?"

Now write your answer in the blank below:

"Just keep _____."

Week 48:

If the allotted time has passed and the project is not done, outline a plan for what remains.

Benjamin Franklin: "Dost thou love life? Then do not squander time; for that's the stuff life is made of."

Don't berate yourself and don't beat yourself up. If the day is over and you've not done what you had planned to do, get a jump start on tomorrow by sketching out your plan for completing what now remains incomplete. Psychologically, you'll feel that you've made an inroad into the leftover assignment. The day will begin better for you if its destination is charted.

This transition sketch need not be complicated—just a few notes so you can pick up where you were forced to leave off.

Action Questions

1. How would you describe yourself as a planner?

_____

_____

_____

_____

2. Uncompleted projects can sometimes drive us to complete them just by virtue of the fact that we weren't able to bring closure to them when we wished to. Why do you think this is so?

_____

_____

_____

_____

Do It Now!

While guilt can be a powerful tool in your self-improvement program, you can overdo its usefulness if you're not careful. If for example, you have "chunked" a large project and planned on finishing one part of it today, don't scold yourself excessively if you don't complete it. There may be very good reasons why you didn't. It's more important that you *began* it.

When you're tempted to pack up a project, even it it's not complete, quickly pull out these questions. If you can answer "yes" to two or more, you should put the work away and not think about it until tomorrow.

1. _____ Were there good reasons why it didn't get done?

2. _____ Would you feel comfortable explaining its delay to your boss?

3. _____ Did you make at least some progress on it today?

4. _____ Is its completion of relatively little importance in the grand scheme of things?

5. _____ Have you jotted down a plan for carrying over to tomorrow what didn't get done today?

Week 49:

Make a list of the reasons why you procrastinate and try to eliminate one every week.

Octavio Paz: "We are condemned to kill time: Thus we die bit by bit."

The unexamined life, so the ancient Greeks asserted, is not worth living. By Week 49, however, you've spent a considerable amount of time examining your life and the way you live it. Nonetheless, engage in yet another self-scrutiny: list the reasons behind your procrastination proclivity.

Each time you procrastinate or are *tempted* to procrastinate, make a note of the circumstances that led you to act or feel this way. When your list has ten to twenty items on it, start to eliminate the negative behaviors one at a time.

Action Questions

1. Consider the psychological underpinnings of your own procrastination behavior. What might they be?

_____

_____

_____

_____

_____

_____

2. How serious are you about wanting to improve?

_____

_____

_____

Do It Now!

The reasons behind procrastination are often legitimate, although they are also often based on ill-founded fears. One important question to ask yourself about your pattern of procrastination is:

> "How do you procrastinate? What exactly do you *do* when you don't do what you should do?"

Sensitize yourself to your daily behaviors. When you catch yourself in the middle of an escapist behavior, pull yourself out of that mode and into a more productive one.

Week 50:

Realize the greatest control you have is on the time of the future. You have no control over the past and little control over the present.

Herbert George Wells: "In England we have come to rely upon a comfortable time lag of fifty years or a century intervening between the perception that something ought to be done and a serious attempt to do it."

Introspection is an uncomfortable process for many people. Without it, though, we lend support to the popular saying: "If you always do what you've always done, you'll always be what you already are."

Being better than you are means looking at what needs improvement, then acting upon your assessed needs.

Action Questions

1. What are some of your biggest regrets about the poor way you've used time during your life?

_____

_____

_____

_____

_____

_____

2. How do you feel at this point about your efforts to defeat procrastination?

_____

_____

_____

_____

_____

_____

Do It Now!

The learning curve required for new practices to become ingrained shortens as we repeat specific behaviors and as we intensify our efforts to include them in our daily patterns. By now you are probably quite adept at isolating those actions that are useful and those that are useless in terms of optimizing the time of your life.

Use the following Useful/Useless Chart several times a week as you continue to sharpen your skills. On the left, record the actions that helped you save time or helped you move toward completion of projects. On the right, list the things that wasted your time or that did not prove to be productive.

Useful/Useless Chart

These things are *Useful*　　　　**These things are *Useless***

in my efforts to fight procrastination:

_____	_____
_____	_____
_____	_____
_____	_____
_____	_____
_____	_____
_____	_____
_____	_____
_____	_____

Week 51:

If an urgent situation pulls you away from what you're doing, ask yourself, "On which of these two priorities would my time be better spent?"

Henry Kissinger: "There can't be a crisis next week. My schedule is already full."

To be sure, you can't be in two places at once. Nor can you do two things at once (unless one of them is a mindless task). Life really is a matter of making choices about time.

All too often, we let the demands of others strip us of the opportunity to deliberate and then choose. The simple question, written in boldface above, should assist you in determining whether or not you should temporarily put aside the task you've undertaken is called for.

Action Questions

1. Joseph M. Juran once observed that some people are so busy putting out fires they don't hear the alarm signals going off. In your own life/career/organization, what alarms are being sounded but not being heard?

_____

_____

_____

_____

_____

2. How would you describe the urgencies of your life?

_____

_____

_____

_____

_____

_____

Do It Now!

Sometimes, despite your best efforts, you have to procrastinate because an equally or more important project competes for your time. For one full week, keep track of the crises or urgencies that pull you away from your best intentions. List those "crises" in the spaces provided below.

At the end of the week, review the list and place the letters "MS" beside those items that proved to be more like match sticks than dynamite in terms of their destructive potential. Write the letters "SE" beside those items that someone else really could have handled. Next, write the letter "R" next to those items that come up repeatedly. Finally, write "PI" beside those items that wouldn't be crises if their processes were improved.

Then scan the list. The items with two or more sets of letters beside them are the ones that offer the greatest potential for being controlled.

1. _____

_____

_____

2. _____

_____

_____

3. _____

_____

_____

4. _____

_____

_____

5. _____

_____

_____

6. _____

_____

_____

7. _____

_____

_____

8. _____

_____

_____

9. _____

_____

_____

10. _____

_____

_____

11. _____

_____

_____

12. _____

_____

_____

13. _____

_____

_____

14. _____

_____

_____

15. _____

_____

_____

16. _____

_____

_____

17. _____

_____

_____

18. _____

_____

_____

19. _____

_____

_____

20. _____

_____

_____

Week 52:
Determine your view of time.

Anonymous: "There is no present like the time."

If you find yourself constantly checking the clock, it may be that time is not on your side. You may be viewing it as the enemy instead of as the enabler that it really is. Time properly spent will enable you to get done what should be done. It will even allow you to use its "spares" or "leftovers" to entertain yourself.

Time is what our heroes use to define their roles in life. Einstein used time to study relativity, Mother Theresa to help the unfortunate, and Martin Luther King to advance civil rights. In a sense, time is an equal-opportunity employer: it gives all of us the same amount.

Action Questions

1. What forces in your life so far have shaped your view of time?

_____

_____

_____

_____

_____

_____

2. If you were asked to deliver a commencement address at a nearby school, what advice would you give the graduates concerning time?

_____

_____

_____

_____

_____

_____

_____

_____

_____

Do It Now!

Which of the following statements comes closest to your own view? (Choose only one.) #_____

1. I view time as a statement of my self-esteem.

2. I view time as an unlimited resource.

3. I view time as a precious commodity.

4. I view time as a curse.

5. I would rather have time than money.

Probe your psyche a bit now and explain why you chose what you did.

_____

_____

_____

_____

_____

Use the space below to specify how you will use the time of your life from this point forward:

_____

_____

_____

_____

_____

_____

_____

_____

Bibliography & Suggested Reading

Blanchard, Kenneth, and Johnson, Spencer. *The One Minute Manager.* New York: William Morrow, 1982.

Burka, Jane. *Procrastination: Why You Do It, What to Do About It.* Reading, Massachusetts: Addison-Wesley, 1983.

Ellis, Albert. *Overcoming Procrastination: Or How to Think and Act Rationally in Spite of Life's Inevitable Hurdles.* New York: New American Library, 1979.

Fiore, Neil. *The Now Habit: A Strategic Program for Overcoming Procrastination and Enjoying Guilt-Free Play.* New York, St. Martin's Press, 1989.

Frank, Milo. *How to Run a Successful Meeting in Half the Time.* New York: Simon & Schuster, 1989.

Granger, Virginia. *How You Can Move Beyond Procrastination.* Tempe, AZ: Moving On Publishers, 1991.

Porat, Frieda. *Creative Procrastination: Organizing Your Own Life.* San Francisco, CA: Harper & Row, 1980.

Smith, Hyrum. *The 10 Natural Laws of Successful Time and Life Management: Proven Strategies for Increased Productivity and Inner Peace.* New York: Warner Books, 1994.

Available From SkillPath Publications

Self-Study Sourcebooks

Climbing the Corporate Ladder: What You Need to Know and Do to Be a Promotable Person *by Barbara Pachter and Marjorie Brody*

Coping With Supervisory Nightmares: 12 Common Nightmares of Leadership and What You Can Do About Them *by Michael and Deborah Singer Dobson*

Defeating Procrastination: 52 Fail-Safe Tips for Keeping Time on Your Side *by Marlene Caroselli, Ed.D.*

Discovering Your Purpose *by Ivy Haley*

Going for the Gold: Winning the Gold Medal for Financial Independence *by Lesley D. Bissett, CFP*

Having Something to Say When You Have to Say Something: The Art of Organizing Your Presentation *by Randy Horn*

The Innovative Secretary *by Marlene Caroselli, Ed.D.*

Mastering the Art of Communication: Your Keys to Developing a More Effective Personal Style *by Michelle Fairfield Poley*

Organized for Success! 95 Tips for Taking Control of Your Time, Your Space, and Your Life *by Nanci McGraw*

A Passion to Lead! How to Develop Your Natural Leadership Ability *by Michael Plumstead*

P.E.R.S.U.A.D.E.: Communication Strategies That Move People to Action *by Marlene Caroselli, Ed.D.*

Productivity Power: 250 Great Ideas for Being More Productive *by Jim Temme*

Promoting Yourself: 50 Ways to Increase Your Prestige, Power, and Paycheck *by Marlene Caroselli, Ed.D.*

Proof Positive: How to Find Errors Before They Embarrass You *by Karen L. Anderson*

Risk-Taking: 50 Ways to Turn Risks Into Rewards *by Marlene Caroselli, Ed.D. and David Harris*

Stress Control: How You Can Find Relief From Life's Daily Stress *by Steve Bell*

The Technical Writer's Guide *by Robert McGraw*

Total Quality Customer Service: How to Make It Your Way of Life *by Jim Temme*

Write It Right! A Guide for Clear and Correct Writing *by Richard Andersen and Helene Hinis*

Handbooks

The ABC's of Empowered Teams: Building Blocks for Success *by Mark Towers*

Assert Yourself! Developing Power-Packed Communication Skills to Make Your Points Clearly, Confidently, and Persuasively *by Lisa Contini*

For more information, call 1-800-873-7545.